God loves you like crazy. Life is too short to worry about anything else.

Based on the quotes of Scott Fetterolf.

Clark Gerhart, Editor

Contributing Authors
Chelsea D'Albero
Seth Fetterolf
Brooke Gerhart
Clark Gerhart
Chuck Humphrey
Lindsay Landis
Brad Travelpiece
Colleen Travelpiece

Advisory Team
Brenda Fetterolf
Seth Fetterolf
Brooke Gerhart

Printed in the United States of America.
First printing, 2019.

ISBN: 978-0-578-58570-3

Graphic Design by Brooke Gerhart

Published by Clark Gerhart
112 State Route 93
Hazleton, PA 18202

www.clarkgerhart.com
www.outrageousloveofanotherkind.com

Praise for Outrageous Love

"I have often heard our lives referred to as our dash, that small piece of punctuation between our birth date and death date on a memorial stone or plaque or program. For some individuals we have known, that dash should be in bold. For a more select few, that small dash is woefully inadequate to summarize the impact of a life well-lived for the cause of Christ. Such is the case for my friend and colleague, Scott Fetterolf. His dash remains so pronounced it continues to speak from beyond his triumphant entry into heaven, because it was never about his own voice. It was about His voice that emanates from, as Scott would say, 'an outrageous love of another kind.' The words in this tome are a rare gift to those of us still here on earth, just as his friendship remains a rare gift to those of us who knew him well."

Dr. Peter W. Teague
President, Lancaster Bible College, Capital
Seminary and Graduate School, Lancaster, PA

"I had the opportunity and privilege to get to know Scott through the process of Emmanuel Bible Chapel joining LCBC Church. The impact and influence Scott had on my life runs too deep to be forgotten. However, Outrageous Love honors Scott in such a way that it helps to keep my memories vivid and alive – I can still hear him speak, feel his 'man hug' and sense him with me still as we conquer the next hill in ministry together. The way Scott adored his wife, Bren, and how he lovingly interacted with his friends, family, partners in ministry and others continues to inspire me. I miss Scott a ton, but this book helps bring a smile to my face as I ponder all the moments we shared. This is an outrageous tribute to a tremendous friend. Thank you to the family members and friends who contributed to this book – I am grateful for how you captured his messages in your words, and for sharing how Scott influenced your lives – To God be the glory!!"

Tim Barley, Sr.
Director of Expansion and Liaison to the Scott J.
Fetterolf Memorial Scholarship at Lancaster Bible
College, LCBC Church, Manheim, PA

Appreciation

I would like to thank Rick Conrad from Kingdom Collaborations for his help in editing both the grammar and theology in this manuscript. Without his input we could not have attained the final level of quality in this book.

A huge “Thank you!” goes out to all of the authors – especially to those who never thought of themselves as authors before committing their thoughts to paper for this project – who spent so much time and energy writing out their entries and then enduring the editing, re-editing and re-re-editing steps that go into writing a book. Your hard work made this happen.

And I want to express my gratitude to Barb Albertson and Corinne Makely for doing the final proofread. When my head was spinning and I couldn’t possibly read the manuscript again, these two swept in to clean up the remaining mistakes and typos that I knew I was missing.

Meet the Authors

Chelsea D'Albero is Ministry Coordinator for LCBC-Lebanon and lives in Lebanon, PA. Scott encouraged and inspired her to reach for and attain her career in ministry.

Seth Fetterolf is a Mechanical Engineer. He and his wife and two sons live in Minot, ND. As Scott's son he has had an entire life of hearing Scott's quotes and seeing them lived out.

Brooke Gerhart is the Worship Leader at LCBC-Hazleton and lives in Conyngham, PA. Scott was influential in Brooke entering ministry and mentored him in that role.

Clark Gerhart is a General Surgeon and lives with his wife in Drums, PA. Clark also has a M.A. in Pastoral Ministry and became a close friend of Scott's as they worked together to plant a church in Hazleton, PA that would later become LCBC-Hazleton.

Chuck Humphrey is an EMS Billing Professional who lives with his wife in Berwick, PA. He worked with Scott for many years on the Elder Board of the church that would become LCBC-Columbia/Montour.

Lindsay Landis is a Sales Professional who lives with her husband and two daughters in Drums, PA. Scott was the most influential pastor in Lindsay's life.

Brad Travelpiece is the LCBC-Hazleton Campus Pastor and lives with his wife in Hazleton, PA. Brad grew up with Scott as his pastor. He mentored Brad while in youth ministry and later as a campus pastor.

Colleen Travelpiece is the Guest Experience Coordinator at LCBC-Columbia/Montour. She lives in Wapwallopen, PA with her husband. Colleen worked alongside Scott for many years as Pastor's Assistant.

God loves you like crazy. Life is too short to worry about anything else.

Based on the quotes of
Scott Fetterolf

Preface

Remembering Scott Fetterolf

It is often difficult to put into words the feelings that surround the loss of a friend or loved one. But when that friend or loved one also happens to be a husband, a father, a son, a brother, as well as a pastor, a teacher and a church leader who seems (at least to us) to have been taken "before his time" and while "still in his prime" – all words seem to fall far short of adequate.

Fortunately, when that loved one also happens to be a son of God and a follower of Jesus Christ it is possible for our mourning to turn to joy. Such is the case with Scott Fetterolf.

From my vantage point as a friend and co-worker with Scott, Scott was a man whose life goal was to make as much of an impact as possible in this life on earth – and then enjoy the party for eternity once he was in heaven.

Scott lived his life with an eternal perspective. He was very much aware that this earth was not his home. Which is why he was often heard saying, "When I die, don't cry for me – instead, throw me a party – because I will be partying in heaven."

Scott could say this because he had no doubts in his mind about where he would spend eternity. Scott whole-heartedly believed that for a son or daughter of God there is nothing better than death because death marks our entry into heaven and eternity with God our heavenly Father.

Scott truly believed that as a follower of Jesus Christ, death is the ultimate good news. So strong was this belief that after the death of his mentor Dr. Gil Peterson, Scott wrote an article about his relationship with Gil. And Scott titled his article, My Friend Died Last Weekend: That's Great News!

Those closest to Scott knew that Scott's love for Jesus was real – it was not just a show. The father of three boys, Scott's sons said, "Dad had a very strict set of priorities. God first. Then mom. Then us kids.

And if something didn't involve one of those three things – God, Mom, or us kids – then Dad didn't do it."

Then for good measure the boys added this nugget about their dad: "Dad ran his life like a sprint. He didn't do things half-heartedly – he only knew one speed – and that was all out!"

But when it comes to describing Scott's passions in life, perhaps Scott's mom said it best in a comment she posted in her private journal. She wrote, "If Scott had known the number of his days it seems unlikely he could have lived his life more effectively, or left a better image in our minds and hearts of what the love of God looks like. He was so focused on the greater joy to come." – Roda Fetterolf

I remember the first few times that Scott spoke at LCBC Church (Lives Changed By Christ) – he was not well received. "Too raw," "Too direct," "Too passionate" were just a few of the comments made. But as time went on, he grew on our church – he became a favorite. And rarely does a month go by without someone telling me how much they still miss Scott.

It is my hope that as we take in the words and pages that follow, some of Scott's passion for Jesus will rub off on us. It would be a great benefit to each of us if we captured even just a thimble full of Scott's hope and excitement for an eternity in heaven with our heavenly Father!

Dr. David Ashcraft
Senior Pastor, LCBC Church
Manheim, PA

Foreword

My Father's Message

God gifted my dad to be a communicator. Whether sitting with one or two people on our back porch or speaking to thousands on a Sunday morning, he had an uncanny ability to connect with his audience. And no matter the setting, his message was consistent. First, that God loves you like crazy and that there's nothing you can do to change that. Second, that life is way too short and eternity way too long to get caught up in earthly things. An understanding of those two truths makes every follower of Christ a powerful ambassador for the Kingdom of God.

This collection of devotions was written by a group of folks who have been impacted by that message. My prayer for you as you read this book is that those truths would sink deep into your heart and bear great fruit. That the finality of your relationship to God would bring you peace and free you to run hard after Him with joy in your heart.

Seth Fetterolf
Mechanical Engineer
Minot, ND

Introduction

The Quotes of Scott Fetterolf

My close friend, mentor and pastor, Scott Fetterolf, died unexpectedly December 12, 2017. He went to bed in Berwick, PA and woke up in heaven. He left behind stunned family, friends and tens of thousands of people connected with LCBC Church where he pastored. Scott got his wish. He led a wonderful life, impacting others, but did not linger in a world he knew was not his home.

Scott and I shared a special bond in the nearly identical way we approached life. We thought alike. We emoted alike. We faced similar struggles and reached for similar goals. When we talked we understood each other. We both knew we could share our struggles together and always receive support, never condemnation. That kind of friendship is a rare thing to find, at least for me. I am blessed to have been able to call Scott a friend. As a friend I want to memorialize him with this book.

But it is more than just a nice gesture to a friend. Scott was one of the most insightful men I have ever known. He had a gift of communicating complex spiritual principles in a way that was understandable and applicable. He was direct and challenging. He resisted religious pretense and verbiage. He spoke in way that we could hear because he really wanted us to experience what he called God's "outrageous love of another kind" that can truly change lives.

He most impacted me with his constant encouragement to take my eyes off of the temporal and keep my focus on the eternal. "This life is just a dot on a line that represents your existence and stretches to eternity," he would remind me. That is what made Scott so impacting. He was able to condense huge principles down to small, memorable statements. Those are the statements I wish to engrave on these pages as a fitting memorial to a life lived to honor God.

Since Scott influenced so many people, it is only natural that we have many people involved in this project. Multiple authors wrote inspirational readings about how his messages influenced them. I also asked people who were familiar with Scott's teaching to participate in an advisory team and I tasked them with keeping the message of the book a clear representation of Scott's style and purpose.

Each entry begins with a quote from Scott taken from one of his messages, videos, blogs, social media posts, or personal communications with the author. Some of Scott's quotes included great ideas that he adapted from someone else's messages. We made every effort to acknowledge those statements that originated with others. Please accept our sincerest apologies if we failed to identify these previous works and falsely attributed them to Scott.

All of these life-changing ideas originate from the Giver of Truth and are found in His original messages in the Bible. So, we included a scripture reference for each quote. Our own explanations of the concepts and how to apply them are also included.

Our goal is not to give you something pleasant to read and discard. We want to give you clear, straight-talking insights, just like Scott would have. Then, challenge you to identify and eliminate harmful ways of thinking – what Scott and others have called *Stinkin' Thinkin'* – and produce healthier, more productive actions. Since Scott loved the word awesome, we're going to call those *Awesome Actions*.

We hope that you are inspired and grow stronger in your faith and experience more of God's outrageous love in your life just as you would have if these quotes were communicated to you by Scott Fetterolf, himself.

Dr. Clark Gerhart, Editor

Advisory Team
Brenda Fetterolf
Seth Fetterolf
Brooke Gerhart

"Outrageous love of another kind."

Mass shootings are a horrendous plague in our society. Yet, in nearly every incident there is a story of self-sacrificing love. A person runs toward the sounds of gunshots instead of away. Someone dives on top of a friend to shield them from bullets. Another tackles a gunman and loses their life to preserve the lives of others.

I often wonder, if I was in one of those situations, would I respond with that kind of sacrificial love? None of us can say until we are actually hearing the gunshots and feeling the brush of air as bullets fly by. But to save my family, friends or innocent children I'd like to think I would.

The people who actually have done it, though, demonstrated one of the most awesome types of love imaginable. Love that gives itself for another.

But that's not outrageous love.

There's a love more incredible than that. It's love that would take a bullet to save a thief. It would give up life so that a prostitute or drug addict might live. It would choose to serve the sentence of a murderer, so that they could go free.

That's outrageous.

But there is a still greater love. It's an outrageous love of a completely different kind that not only spares wrongdoers of a penalty, it blesses them. It takes the person who had an affair with their spouse and fills their pockets with money to help them start a new life. It takes the person who brutally murders their child and invites them into their home giving them a place to live.

Too shocking? Too graphic? I know. It's outrageous.

And yet that's exactly what God's love has done for us. We claim to be the bride of Christ and yet run after so many other loves. And still, He blesses us. We caused His Son to die a horrible death and still He invites us into relationship.

His love is outrageous. It's a completely different kind of love.

Poets and bards of old, and modern song composers – along with countless greeting card writers – have tried to describe love in words, and they still come up short. The love of a mother for a child. A husband for his wife. Brother for brother. Sister for sister. They are all powerful depictions of love and hard to explain.

Now try to describe the love that God has for us. Go ahead, I'll wait … Still there? … Want to keep trying? … Can't really do it, can you? Paul tells us that God's love is too great to ever fully understand. It's not like any human love we know. It's outrageous. It's a love of another kind.

> And may you have the power to understand, as all God's people should, how wide, how long, how high, and how deep his love is. May you experience the love of Christ, though it is too great to understand fully. Then you will be made complete with all the fullness of life and power that comes from God.
>
> Ephesians 3:18-19 (NLT)

That's why Paul prayed that we would understand and experience this incredible love that is too great to fully comprehend.

Loving those who do good to you and punishment for those who don't is easy to understand. That's how humanity works. But God's love is outrageously different. Scott encouraged us to accept God's outrageous love of another kind, even if we couldn't understand it.

Since I can't explain it, I'll just let Scott say it as he did in one of his sermons:

> I'm a big boy, you're a big boy or a big girl. You deserve the consequences of our own choice. I get that. It makes sense. What doesn't make any sense is how much outrageous love of another kind it takes to sacrifice something perfect (Christ) for something not even close to perfect (you and me). Today stop trying to understand this love. It's impossible. Instead accept it. Give up your objections that you are not worthy of God's love. It's true you're not! But while worthiness may be a prerequisite for some types of love, God's love is outrageous. If you have accepted Christ's perfection into your life, God's love for you is perfect. You can do nothing to be more loved. You can do nothing that makes Him love you less.
>
> Get this. Let it sink in. You are fully pleasing to Almighty God. There's nothing you can do to make yourself more pleasing.

Are you hindered by feelings of guilt? Do you feel unworthy of God's love? Does it seem unimaginable that God could love you with your past? Your present? Is it impossible to picture how your life could be a benefit to others? Apparently, you're not getting the outrageous love available to you.

Paul writes in his letter to Christians, just like us, who lived in Rome in his day, that God loved us enough to die for us while we were sinners, long before we got the chance to try and clean up our act on our own. (Romans 5:8) And if that wasn't enough, he bestows gifts on us as well. (Ephesians 4:1) Outrageous. So why would you think you're not loved because of some flaw you have? He loved you *before you knew* about the flaw and *after He knew* about it. And He blessed you with unique gifts that make you valuable to others on top of that.

Take a moment and let that sink it. I know it's hard. That's because it's outrageous and a kind of love we never experience anywhere else. But as you give up trying to understand it and just accept it, that outrageous love of another kind will change your life.

TODAY'S CHALLENGE

1. **Eliminate Stinkin' Thinkin'**
   Do you often think you are unworthy of God's love? Do you feel that you could never be used by God to impact others? Recognize that these feelings are the dead fish that wash up on shore from the toxic waste of wrong ideas about your worth buried in the depths of your thought life. Identify those deeply buried thoughts as wrong when compared to what God says about you.

2. **Initiate Awesome Actions**
   Spend time with God in prayer telling Him about those feelings. Ask for His forgiveness for doubting His love for you. Thank Him for His love despite your shortcomings. Now, and for the rest of your life, tell yourself that you are loved and accepted by God … even if it doesn't make sense. Write notes to remind yourself that you are loved, and that God has a plan for using you – even your failures – to make His love known to other people.

Clark Gerhart

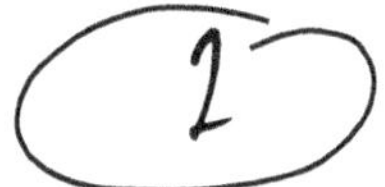

"Invest the dot for the line."

During one of Scott's messages he projected a line all the way across the screen at the front of the auditorium and told us that the line represents 600,000,000 years. After pausing just long enough for us to try to begin to understand the depths of that, he went on to say, "I just couldn't fit a line up there that effectively represented all of eternity." He then showed us a very small dot and said that proportionally that is what an 80-year lifespan would look like compared to 600,000,000 years. (You can find a mini-version at the top of the page and on the cover of this book.) Other speakers have used long ropes stretched across the room. I've heard people compare a speck on the sidewalk next to the Empire State Building. The point is the same. Right now is tiny. Eternity is big.

That's a good thing because right now can be pretty crappy sometimes and putting it in perspective helps.

Many times, Scott and I would sit and process the crappier parts of life … the good ones, too, but they usually took less processing. The best place for us to process was Jackie's, a little greasy spoon breakfast spot midway between the two church campuses he was overseeing. Now, don't get me wrong, I say greasy spoon as a compliment. The food tasted good and filled you up … nothing on the menu ever included kale … the eggs were never in quiche form. Scott couldn't do quiche. He said it was the name. He couldn't get past wondering, "Why don't they call quiche egg pie?" If you're ever in town stop at Jackie's.

Some of what we processed were the ups and downs of our church campus. Some days the ministry was like driving a convertible up the coastal highway … the sun on your face … wind in your hair. Awesome! Other days, it was like being in a car crash test, smashing into a wall. On those days when I was the crash dummy, Scott would remind me that it was all just a dot. There are much bigger things – eternal things – happening. Don't let the dot distract you from the rest of the line.

And let's face it, the dot of our lives will be full of ups and downs. In his book *A Million Miles in a Thousand Years*, Donald Miller encourages us to see the twists and turns we face are simply making an interesting story of our lives. Like a good movie, a good life story occasionally includes the hero screeching his car around corners nearly plummeting off the cliff. It's exciting, not devastating because you know that somehow, he'll survive. Because he's the hero. He'll win in the end.

That is the story of our lives, too. We know we win in the end. So, we can sit back and excitedly wait to see how our next scary scene turns out. Of course, when you are up on two wheels and staring down the side of a cliff, that reality is a little tough to remember. So, it is at those times in life when we need to remind ourselves that life is a long line that lasts into eternity and the heart-wrenchingly difficult parts are just a few scenes out of a movie. In fact, they are making your life story better. So, during the tough times, lean in and push through to victory ahead. *Invest the dot for the line.*

Scott also reminded us of another reality: Investing the small amount of time we have on earth in spiritually valuable ways pays off big time when you receive the huge reward that is heaven. So, invest the dot for the line. Stop spending so much time working hard to make your life here more comfortable. Spend a little more time working hard to make other peoples' eternity more comfortable, even if it makes life here less comfortable for you.

Paul gave the Colossian Christians similar advice. Our new reality is in Christ, he explained, and in heaven where He sits next to God. I'm sure he encouraged them, when life gets tough … and those early Christians had it pretty tough … to keep thinking about eternity and not your hardships now, here on earth. Whatever you sacrifice now is just a dot compared to the infinite line of riches you will receive in heaven. So, *invest the dot for the line.*

We may not face the same violent persecution that the first century Christians faced, but it is still hard to endure ridicule when we are scoffed at for spending time at church instead of on the golf course. Or, when we are treated like we are uninformed or unintelligent when we adhere to biblical, moral standards that are not seen as progressive. Or, when it seems like the ruthless and cut-throat of this world succeed. But we don't have to worry when we sacrifice the supposedly good things of this world. They're just a dot. And, it is always a good deal to *invest the dot for the line.*

TODAY'S CHALLENGE

1. **Eliminate Stinkin' Thinkin'**
   Think for a moment about how much time you spend thinking about your own needs and wants. Hold that thought. Now look through your calendar and checkbook … figuratively will be fine. You don't have to get out your calendar app and online bank account. How much time and money do you spend just surviving in this world? Depressing isn't it? When you get sucked into the self-centered, problem-focused mindset, remind yourself that everything you struggle with right now is just a dot. There is a whole lot more of life – an eternity full – out there that is important. And it is being crowded out by the far less important but much louder stuff screaming details in your face right now. Draw a dot and a line on a 3x5 card and stick it to your mirror, or in your car. Or, if you really need reminding tattoo it on your arm, like I did. Keep the eternity focused mindset visible and in front of your thinking any way you can.

2. **Initiate Awesome Actions**
   You need to set time aside to forcibly tear your mind free from the immediate temporal issues and spend time focusing on eternal issues, the most important of which are the only thing that will accompany you into eternity – other people. Plan to set aside some of the time in your schedule regularly to invest some of your dot in eternal purposes. This may mean setting aside your prayer list that is full of requests for how you want God to make your life better and regularly pray for others. It might also mean finding a project where you can volunteer to invest time in other's lives.

Clark Gerhart

"Be who you are. Remember to whom you belong. The rest is just details."

On the way to school… be who you are. Before a football game… be who you are. Advice for a big decision… be who you are. I could never count the number of times Dad said to my brothers and me, "Be who you are. Remember to whom you belong. The rest is just details." It's the wisdom that finds its way into every situation. It drove me nuts as a kid. "I know, I know! Be who I am. But how does that help me in everyday life?"

I've come to learn that, like it or not, it just does.

So, like The Who asked in the 70s, "Who are you? (Who, who? Who, who?)" How do YOU answer that question? Are you a wife or a husband? A son or a daughter? A teacher, a doctor, a plumber? An optimist? A lover or a fighter? If you're like me, it takes a while to answer that question. You're lots of things. But whether you define yourself by your position in your family, the things you do, the things you love, or the way you think, we all define ourselves by the way we relate to things external to us. It's part of the human condition.

There is One of Whom that is not true. In the book of Exodus, God is getting ready to introduce Himself to the nation of Israel. He starts with Moses, the man He chose to be His messenger. God shows up in Moses' life by making a torch out of a shrub and commanding him to go free His people. Afraid, Moses tries to get himself out of it. He asks God, "What if I tell the people 'God sent me' and they ask, 'Yeah?

What's His name'?" Moses' question is feeble, but God's answer is earth shaking. He says, "I AM".

You see, God doesn't define Himself by a relationship to anything else. He simply *is*. He *is* holy. He *is* just. He *is* good. None of us can ever answer like that. I might be able to say I'm a good friend or a good golfer, but I can't say I AM good. We define ourselves by the way we relate in the world. We can describe God similarly because He relates in the world, but He is also the I AM. He doesn't need anything else to define Himself. God *is* the being by which all other things are defined. Everything else needs God in order to be. Including you and me.

As you believe in the name and work of Jesus, God says that you are his perfect son or daughter (1 John 3:1-3; Hebrews 10:12-14). Is that who you are? Then be who you are! We'll spend our lives learning the depth and joy of being His children. For now, know that every other relationship to every other person and every other thing, all mean nothing compared to your relationship with The One who defines all. The One who says you are precious, honored, loved and *His* (Isaiah 43:1-3).

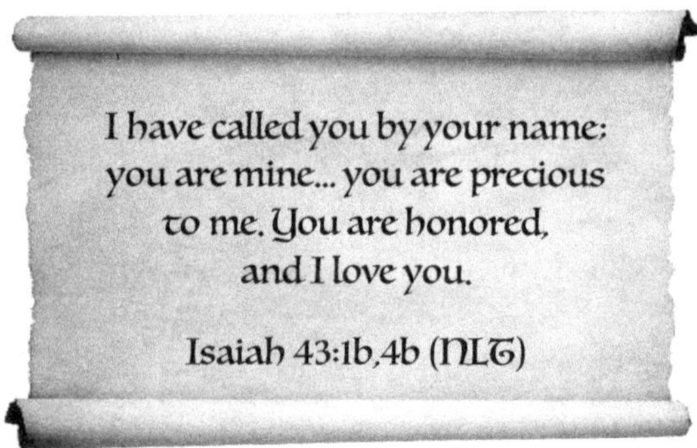

In John 10:28-29 Jesus says, "I give them eternal life and they will never perish. No one can snatch them out of My hand. My Father who has given them to Me is greater than all. No one can snatch them out of my Father's hand." *Remember to whom you belong.* Your identity lies squarely and securely in the hands of One and only One. No challenge or accusation or snide comment from an enemy can touch you.

If we are children of God, much loved and secure in His hand, what then? Why does that matter on the way to school? On the way to work?

Meeting with a big client? Deciding on a career path? The answer is: None of that affects who you are. *It is just details.*

As secure sons and daughters of the King we know that, regardless of the outcomes of daily circumstances our eternity is already decided. We know that our Father loves us no matter what happens. Nobody else's opinion matters. Because of that, secure sons and daughters get to set big, hairy, audacious goals. It doesn't matter if we fail (and maybe we won't) because failing doesn't change who we are. We get to run hard after what God puts in front of us, not worried that we might fall. We get to shout and dance and sing like nobody is watching because Someone *is* watching. And he loves it! So go! Dream big, run hard and dance like a fool.

As I write this, I'm glancing over at a baby monitor that's watching my five-month-old son as he naps. He'll be stirring soon and probably start to cry. He'll cry because he's alone and doesn't yet understand that I'm in the next room. Or maybe because he's hungry (again) and doesn't remember that every time he's hungry his mom or I feed him. His world isn't very complicated right now but honestly, the things I struggle with aren't that different. Sometimes I feel like God is far away because he is out of sight and I don't know when he'll be back. Sometimes I worry too much about progress in my career, or for provision for my family when I don't need to. After all, I know I am God's son and he'll care for me like I care for my son.

At five months old life is pretty simple, but it will get harder. And I can't wait to tell my son what my dad told me. Because no matter where you are in life, the answer is the same: Be who you are. Remember to whom you belong. The rest is just details.

TODAY'S CHALLENGE

1. **Eliminate Stinkin' Thinkin'**
   Are there times when you think negatively about yourself? Do you worry about what someone else is thinking about you? If so, it is time to eliminate those thoughts and replace them with the truth that you are a son or daughter of God and loved deeply by Him. And like a loving father, he doesn't disown you or withhold his love and favor when you fail. He lovingly walks with you through times of struggle, helping you learn and grow stronger. Let that truth impact the way you think and feel about yourself. You can be confident and secure in your relationship with God because of who He said you are.

2. **Initiate Awesome Actions**
   Start your day tomorrow by thanking God for being your dad. Reflect on how He loves regardless of life's details. Keep that at the forefront of your mind and live out every action in light of it. Write down in a journal your thoughts and Bible verses on God's fatherly love for you. Reflect on those thoughts when the details of life make it tough to remember who you really are.

Seth Fetterolf

"Earthly stress can't stand in the face of an eternal perspective."

In the epic movie (at least I think it's epic), The Princess Bride (20th Century Fox, 1987), the hero, Wesley, tells Princess Buttercup, "Life is pain, Highness. Anyone who tells you differently is selling something." While the movie is a comedy, the truth of the statement is no joke … life after the Garden of Eden is full of stress. No more strolling through the orchard plucking a fruit salad for lunch. Now you have to get a job if you want to eat. Then there's illness, famine, war and – equally distressing – cable news to put up with! (ugh!) So, I'm here to tell you Princess, life is full of pain.

Maybe you were hoping Christianity would eliminate all stress? Well, if Wesley's quote is true, I have another for you: "Christian life also has pain. Anyone who tells you differently is looking for a donation." Christ said it this way, "In this world you will have tribulation." (John 16:33) Even for those of us who follow Christ, life is hard.

So, how do we overcome stress? There are lots of books and seminars on how to manage stress. Use those tips when you can. But when problems aren't so easily resolved, the key is to see past them to an eternal perspective.

Christ taught this to his first disciples while rowing across the sea of Galilea in a small fishing boat, when they encountered a storm that threatened to send them all to a watery death. To us it is a wonderful Bible story. But if you were in that boat … like Mark was, who tells us this story … you would have endured a terrifying night of darkness, buffeting wind, flashing lightening, and billowing swells which threatened to capsize the small craft carrying your life in its small hull.

Or did it? Did the little boat hold their lives? In the next few moments Jesus would show them that their lives were more than just what was happening in the moment.

More important than the storm was the disciples' response to the storm. When the disciples finally included Jesus in their struggles, all they could say was, "Don't you care that we drown?" I do the same, and maybe you, too. I scurry around my sinking ship, trimming sails, bailing water and rowing like crazy, until I am going under. Then I use my last breath to question God's love for me instead of calling out in faith. I see only the waves and never ask the guy who controls them for an answer.

> But soon a fierce storm came up. High waves were breaking into the boat, and it began to fill with water. Jesus was sleeping at the back of the boat with his head on a cushion. The disciples woke him up, shouting, "Teacher, don't you care that we're going to drown?" When Jesus woke up, he rebuked the wind and said to the waves, "Silence! Be still!" Suddenly the wind stopped, and there was a great calm. Then he asked them, "Why are you afraid? Do you still have no faith?"
>
> Mark 4:37-40 (NLT)

Jesus makes clear that the antidote to fear is faith. I generally hate cheesy church signs but one I saw was profound. It read, "No faith, no peace. Know faith, know peace." It's true. If we can look past the waves of our temporal lives to see God's eternal perspective on our problems and walk with Him in faith every step of the way, we will have peace in the midst of the storm.

Many of life's storms are designed with an eternal purpose of teaching us more about God. God allowed the disciples to face a near drowning event to grow in relationship with Him. I can just imagine the disciples as they finished pulling the boat on shore, Jesus is walking ahead up the beach, and they turn gapping at each other, shaking their heads and asking, "Who is this guy? Did you just see the wind and waves obey Him, or was it just me?"

Who is he, indeed?!

He's the guy who controls all of life's storms.

If you stand apart in the midst of stress and curse God for your misery you will never really know who He could be to you. But if you run to Him, nudge His shoulder, and rouse Him to your aid in the midst of the storm, He will guide you through. He will be a teacher, friend, mentor, father … and so much more. You will surely grow in relationship with Him, which is His greatest goal.

This doesn't mean that all your storms will end well. Sometimes ships sink. Sometimes He calms the storm and sometimes He calms his child. (Shoot! I think I just quoted another church sign!) His words, "Peace. Be still," (Mark 4:39, KJV) can just as easily be spoken to you and me as they can be directed at the winds.

If you only have faith when the seas are calm you have no faith at all. If that's not already a church sign it should be! The hymn *It is Well* was written by Horatio G. Spafford after he lost his four children in a shipwreck crossing the Atlantic in 1873. While later making the same trip, at the exact spot where his children died, he penned the words, "When peace like a river attendeth my way, When sorrows like sea billows roll. Whatever my lot, Thou hast taught me to say, it is well, it is well with my soul." He never could have imagined that his tragedy at sea would encourage millions of people for hundreds of years. But he could trust that the One who controlled the waves had an eternal purpose. And, it was well with his soul.

TODAY'S CHALLENGE

1. **Eliminate Stinkin' Thinkin'**
   When troubles arise are you prone to asking God, "Why aren't you fixing this problem?" or maybe, "Why do you let other people always win and I always fail?" If you have trouble seeing this thinking as stinkin', try picturing a toddler and hearing those same questions in a child's whine. Yeah, it kind of stinks, doesn't it? It is time to react to God more maturely. Resolve to see the problems in life as part of the natural forces that govern this sin-sick world just as naturally and as inevitably as the weather buffets us at times. Instead of crying that God is unfair or unloving when you experience problems, see them as a challenge that you can face together with Him.

2. **Initiate Awesome Actions**
   Find the modern version of *It is Well* by Bethel Music. In that version we are reminded that, "The waves and wind still know His name." After meditating on that, make a declaration that you will trust that God has an eternal purpose for whatever you are going through. Write it down and post it someplace you'll see daily as a constant reminder. Talk it over with a trusted friend, and remind each other when the storms come, to run to the One who controls the waves.

Clark Gerhart

"Nothing about you that matters is at stake today."

Recently I was driving my Kindergartner to school, as I do every day. (Joys of being a stay-at-home mom!) My six-year-old was unusually quiet in the backseat, so I asked her what she was thinking about. She told me she was really hoping they were not going to do computers today. This baffled me. The same kid that would be glued to the tablet every chance that she got, who asked to play games on my phone and laptop constantly, was dreading computer lab? So, I prodded further, asking if something happened during computer time.

Her response broke my heart. She described how during computer time, there is a little clock in the bottom corner that counts down, and if you do not get a 100 to appear on the screen after you have done all the math and reading questions, you have to try again and again until you get a perfect score.

That's it? This didn't seem like such a big deal. So you try again if you don't get a 100% on the first try? But before I responded to her distress, I looked in the rearview mirror and I saw tense posture and furrowed brow that looked all too familiar. I see that same face in the bathroom mirror every day.

I'm not sure if it is the "firstborn child syndrome," as we affectionately refer to it in our house, (a house full of firstborns), but somehow the fear of failure is already deeply instilled in her.

I tell her that she doesn't have to be perfect on the first try. She is there to learn and her best effort is all that we, and her teacher, expect. Her facial expression doesn't change much. "OK," she says quietly.

I watch her walk into school and realize that there may not be a visible clock counting down, but I feel the same pressure. Have I taken care of all the household details? Have I met the physical, emotional and spiritual needs of my kids, husband and extended family…let alone my own self-care? The day has run out, and I wonder to myself, *Have I checked 100% of the boxes today? Well, no, probably not. Have I checked enough to be worthy of love? If not – gasp – what will happen to me? And how can I help my daughter with fear of failure when I have not discovered the cure for this malady myself?*

I recall hearing Scott tell similar stories about bringing up three boys. Before a big game, or a presentation at school, whatever they were going to face in the world that day, he would remind them, "Nothing about you that matters is at stake today."

Wait, what?? No spinning clock demanding 100%?

Hearing that was like tasting a caramel macchiato for the first time – a whole new world opened up!

I was finally seeing unconditional love. Failing at the many daily events holds no stake in my worth. I am still loved. Growing up, my parents reinforced my worth. How had I missed this?

Because, I heard it but didn't believe it, and that shaped my reality.

Here's the core concept: *If you believe a lie, it affects you as if it were true.*

In my perfectionism I believed the lie that God (and others for that matter) will not *really* love me if I mess up too many times. And, that lie became my reality. It kept me locked in a prison of fear and doubt. Tragically, I never opened up my hands to receive God's gift of unconditional love.

I don't know what lies you listen to. Maybe you're like me and my daughter thinking that if the score on the screen isn't 100 you're not good enough. Or maybe you believe you are a screw-up because you messed up another relationship or lost another job. Perhaps you believe you are unlovable because you are plagued by addiction, anger or depression. Believe lies like these and they'll bind you like a boa constrictor as if they were true.

To break the power of these lies, you have to hear and believe the truth.

In Isaiah God tells us, "Come to me with your ears wide open," and then, "Listen!" Now, I'm a mom, and I know from experience that when I repeat myself, it means PAY ATTENTION. I think God the Father here is saying, "Listen up kids! In order to receive My unfailing love, you must not only come with hands open ready to receive it, but with ears open ready to hear the truth and believe it! So, LISTEN!" That sounds like God's love is conditional and it's not. His love is freely given to us. But, if we are distracted by the lie that we are unloved, we don't receive the benefit of feeling that love. So, we have to LISTEN UP as God tells us the truth about His love.

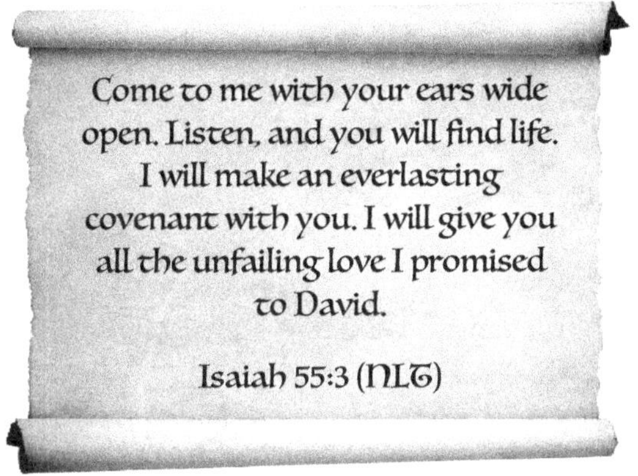

Here is the truth God speaks to us in Isaiah: I make an everlasting promise to give you unfailing love. Love that can't fail, forever. THAT is the truth. Choose to accept it and it will affect you. Your worth is no longer tied to your actions. It is based on God's love for you. Fear is replaced with peace and safety. Keep the truth of God's unfailing love at hand to remind you when your feet hit the floor in the morning – before you even look in that mirror – that you are loved unconditionally, and *nothing about your worth is at stake today.*

TODAY'S CHALLENGE

1. **Eliminate Stinkin' Thinkin'**
   Fear of failure, and feelings of inadequacy are common mental roadblocks that will stop you in your tracks on the journey of personal growth. The truth that combats these is simply that you are loved and valued regardless of whether you succeed or fail today. But, it is simply not enough to hear something; you must believe it. When you are afraid you don't measure up, choose to accept the truth that your accomplishments or failures do not affect God's unfailing love for you … and that this is all that really matters in the long run.

2. **Initiate Awesome Actions**
   Write down the truth in Isaiah, multiple times if need be. Say it out loud, repeat the truth to your kids, go over it again and again and let the truth take root in your heart. Then go get a caramel macchiato ☺.

Lindsay Landis

"To improve your marriage overnight, stop asking God to make your spouse right for you, and ask Him to make you right for your spouse."

A girl rides off in a white pickup truck with a wild and exciting guy her folks don't approve of, leaving "suds in the bucket" as in the song by Sara Evans. As responsibilities mount, what was exciting becomes a drag. Determined to make a stable relationship work she sets out to change him. Other times it's the guy enthralled by Jon Pardi's "heartache on the dance floor" … the girl that captures his heart during a night of sultry music and dancing. Eventually, he realizes that relationship requires more than great moves at the club. Determined to make a stable relationship work he sets out to change her.

These scenarios so common they write songs about them. The answers seem easy. She wants her wild guy to settle down, sell his truck and get a minivan. He wants his party girl to learn how to communicate with something other than her hips. "If only *they* would change, our marriage would be better," they each think.

Many have given similar advice to those struggling with relationship. Scott would simply say, "To improve your marriage overnight: Stop asking God to make your spouse right for you; ask Him to make you right for your spouse." After over 30 years of marriage, I can tell you that there is only one person in the relationship that you can change: You. And that's hard enough.

Sooooo many times I prayed, "God, search my wife's heart, show her what offends me, and lead her in the everlasting truth that she has to treat me better," in my twisted version of Psalm 139. Okay, maybe not that exactly, but I've definitely prayed something similar. And you may be shocked to find out that no fairy godmother showed up to wave her wand and make my wife into a princess. But then I wasn't always Prince Charming, either.

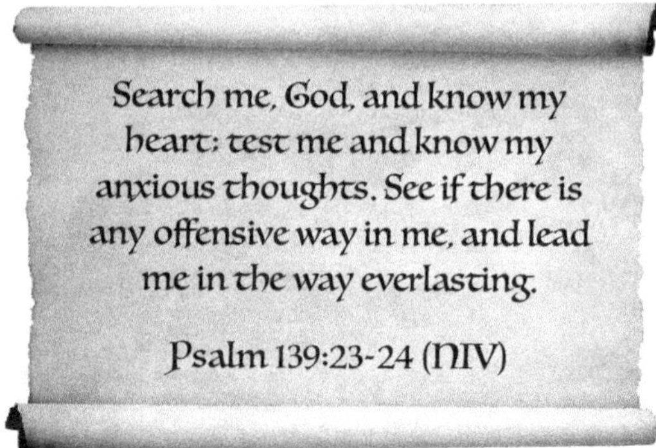

If you're in the same boat and want your marriage, or any other significant relationship, to improve, stop praying for the other person to change. Let's find a better prayer.

The best bet is finding a prayer in scripture and praying it just the way it is. You know God liked the prayer if he included it in the manual of how to do Christianity, the Bible. It's like the Lord's prayer in Matthew 6:9-13. Jesus said, "Pray this way…" So, you can become a prayer warrior overnight by just praying like He said: "God, my Father, you are Holy. Strengthen the work of Your Kingdom on earth, in our country, in my town. Show me Your will so I can take part in it. Give me what I need. Forgive me. Help me to forgive others. Strengthen me against temptation and protect me from evil." Bam! Perfect prayer that God will hear because He wrote it.

Psalm 139 is another prayer in scripture. And it is a great one to pray to improve your relationships. You should pray something like this: "My relationship with my wife really sucks right now. I know I'm focusing mostly on what's wrong with *her*. Could you look through my heart and point out the stuff in *me* that may be adding stress to our communication, then help *me* deal with those things, so *I* can do *my* part in making the relationship better?" Bam! Perfect relationship prayer, automatically heard by God because … you guessed it … He wrote it.

So, if you want to improve your marriage overnight, spend tonight doing some work on *you*. Stop trying to change your spouse. It is wasted energy.

But just because you can't change them doesn't mean they can't be changed. Watching you examine yourself will give most people at least a moment to pause – right after they gain consciousness from passing out from shock – and consider their own actions.

And let's not overlook that God can change them. God has written prayers for you to pray to help your spouse improve, too. Paul prayed for his friends in Ephesus, "That He would grant you, according to the riches of His glory, to be strengthened with power through His Spirit in the inner man." Ephesians 3:16 (NASB) Praying that your spouse gets strengthened in their deep, inner life is huge. So much of our poor communication in marriage comes out of past wounds deep inside that get poked in the course of interacting with another humans, making the old pain flare. Pray that God heals your mate deep inside where those hurts exist. God wrote that prayer. He can't not hear it.

One of the best parts of praying for your spouse is that *you* will hear that prayer. It will get your focus off yourself and your own hurts and open your eyes to theirs. As a result, your interactions will become more empathetic and caring towards them. When that happens, your relationship will change overnight.

TODAY'S CHALLENGE

1. **Eliminate Stinkin' Thinkin'**
   If you think you can solve relationship problems by winning an argument, give up the fight! You've lost already, based on the wrong thinking that arguments can be won by hashing through facts. Arguments are based on looking at the same facts from different perspectives and getting different emotional responses. Most of the time in disagreements people just want their perspective and their feelings heard. Change the focus to listening. Then, once each person feels heard you can better deal with the facts.

2. **Initiate Awesome Actions**
   Stop trying to change your spouse and start praying Psalm 139 for yourself. Then pray for God to heal your spouse inside, not just to selfishly make them treat *you* better, but to make *their* lives better. Pray for things together. Become partners in dealing with problems, not enemies. And here is a very powerful trick: Hold hands while praying. Skin to skin contact releases oxytocin in the blood stream which is a hormone that causes emotional bonding. Try holding hands while fighting – it's almost impossible!

Clark Gerhart

"Normal isn't working. So, choose to be weird."

I'm not sure why so many people want to be normal. If you are the statistically average American, this is you:

You are overweight. And not just "my jeans are too tight" overweight. Seventy percent of us are overweight or obese according to the Centers for Disease Control. And they're the government, so you can trust them.

You carry $9,333 in credit card debt. But it's not entirely your fault. As Dave Ramsey tells us, you're in debt because you pay money you don't have to buy things you don't need to impress people you don't like. So, it's those people's fault – the ones you don't like.

The good news is you have a college degree. The bad news is that you left school owing $37,172 to get job that paid $49,785 leaving you with very little to pay off those loans. So, there's a one out of ten chance you will default.

Fortunately, you have a spouse to comfort you – at least half of you do. Unless you're under thirty then you're almost certainly single because you're a millennial and you are too busy working on selfies to develop strong two-zies – which is a name I just made up for when two people get married. No big deal, though, the first marriage only lasts about eight years anyway.

That's okay, too, because once you're divorced, you'll have more time to commit to your true, life-long commitment – your next tattoo. Currently, the majority of Americans do not have tattoos, only 38% of the 18 to 30-year-old crowd does. But it is fast becoming "normal" up from 24% in 2012. Even many of the (slightly) older folks like me and my Gen-X'ers have tattoos.

At least you have friends. On average you have 338 "friends" on Facebook. You will spend very little time with them, however, because you spend 10 hours and 39 minutes a day – that's right, *a day* – in front of some sort of screen. Not much time left to spend with real humans.

But you're not all bad. Chances are you don't smoke, since only about 15% of us do. And you will eat 19 avocados this year. That's over seven pounds per person! Good job on those healthy choices!

Now if you're concerned that I made all this up, don't be. I got all the statistics from the internet, which means they're true. But don't take the internet's word for it. Just look around you. *Normal* equals being stressed out, over stimulated, disconnected people looking for meaning the only way we know how … through Wi-Fi.

If that's normal, I choose weird.

It really struck me the first time I heard Scott repeat this quote, that originated with Craig Groeschel in his book *Weird: Because Normal Isn't Working* (Zondervan, 2012). Normal – the thing we all tend to strive for – really is *not* all it's cracked up to be!

Matthew, one of the guys that hung out with Jesus tells us that the normal way people tend to go, does not necessarily end up where we want to go. You'll probably recognize the Bible passage that says, "Enter through the narrow gate. For wide is the gate and broad is the road that leads to destruction, and many enter through it. But small is the gate and narrow the road that leads to life, and only a few find it," That is Matthew 7:13-14, today's passage, but in the New International Version, the way many remember it. That's no joke. It's pretty clear. If you follow the normal crowd down the wide highway you end up in a bad place. Search hard for a little gate that's hidden along a hillside at the end of a narrow winding trail, and you find the good place.

I like the way The Message paraphrases this verse in Matthew to show just what we see in our society today, "The market is flooded with surefire, easygoing formulas for a successful life that can be practiced in your spare time." There are so many easy ways to get around our problems today. Just Google it and you'll find a life hack to deal with just about whatever bothers you. But finding life, now and eternally, is not that easy. And if you follow the way everyone else is heading, you'll only get where everyone else is going. There's a whole lot of stressed out people with broken lives traveling that way.

> Don't look for shortcuts to God. The market is flooded with surefire, easygoing formulas for a successful life that can be practiced in your spare time. Don't fall for that stuff, even though crowds of people do. The way to life—to God!—is vigorous and requires total attention.
>
> Matthew 7:13-14 (MSG)

So, what is the right way – I mean the weird way?

If you think the Bible is confusing sometimes, the Biblical answer to this one is clear. Jesus said, "I am the way." Not so hard to figure out. Live like Jesus did. This includes dedicating your life to loving the unlovable, humbly serving others, and helping people find their way back to their Creator.

It is definitely not the easy way, but I can tell you from my own life that if you are willing to follow Jesus down an exit ramp off the broad freeway, He'll lead you down a narrow two-lane that leads to a life based on love. And if you do, you'll start to look a little weird to those up on the interstate headed the opposite direction. When you trust that Jesus loves you with the kind of love He demonstrated when He was on earth, you'll have a sense of peace, which is really strange these days. And as you participate in the work of spreading His Love to others you will really look weird. Who would love others more than themselves, as Jesus instructed us to do? That's crazy!

Normal isn't working, so let's try that kind of weird for a change.

TODAY'S CHALLENGE

1. **Eliminate Stinkin' Thinkin'**
   Challenge yourself with a dose of vulnerable introspection. "Am I looking for happiness in money, success or people's admiration? Am I still left wanting? That's the broad way. It is based on the idea that real peace and satisfaction in life comes from accumulating lots of stuff and lots of followers of Instagram. And it's a stinkin' lie. Unfortunately, it's a falsehood that gets repeated so frequently – literally sent to us in our in-boxes everyday – that it is hard to reject entirely. But reject it we must if we are to find the narrow gate that leads to true life by following Jesus down a path of love and self-sacrifice.

2. **Initiate Awesome Actions**
   Following Jesus is not easy, but it is also not as complicated as you might believe. It is about love. Discard religiosity and focus your spiritual life on experiencing God's love for yourself and sharing it with others. Start by reading the Gospel of John in the Bible, which describes Jesus's life, and look for ways that he loved people. As you read the rest of the New Testament, appreciate how God loves you instead of looking for rules for living. Now, live out that same love by going out and committing some weird act of kindness for someone today.

Clark Gerhart

"Choose opportunity over security."

"Take Route 11 north into Briar Creek. Turn left at the body shop and drive to the intersection with Route 93 (Orange St.). Go through the intersection and drive to Cemetery Road. Hang left onto Cemetery Road and drive to the "T" intersection. Turn right and look left…the church will be on your left on Kachinka Hollow Road."

Those were the directions I gave to the first person I invited to church sometime after we plugged into our new church. Funny how, thinking back now, I hear my GPS saying "Recalculating" ringing in my ears as I think about those directions now! I remembered thinking, "They'll never find us."

Our church started when a core group of people landed over 30 years prior and camped out to do church. The building, the people… it was all safe, comfortable and *just right.*

Enter Scott Fetterolf as pastor in 2001. To him, nothing was *just right* when it came to The Mission. He believed that a church that isn't growing is really dying and certainly not fulfilling its purpose. Scott saw the bigger picture. There were people who needed to know Jesus and this building wasn't convenient to fit that mission. It was hidden geographically, too small to promote unlimited growth and quickly becoming dated. Scott challenged us to be a hospital for souls and not a Christian club.

One day God showed Scott a vision of our area's promised land in the form of a vacant supermarket perfectly positioned at an intersection where people in 3 counties do life every day. That was a big vision that required change.

The Bible tells us there was another guy that God gave a big vision to. His name was Abram. God took Abram to a place outside his family's encampment one day and showed him the future. On one side was a land that was fertile and on the other side, not so much. God told Abram that day that He would make him the father of a great nation and give him a land on the not-so-fertile side that stretched farther and wider than he could ever begin to imagine. Abram's name would change to Abraham. A subtle change, but one that reflected his change from a father of a single family to a father of a vast nation.

To fulfill this vision, all Abram had to do was uproot his entire family, his livestock and the stuff that went with all of that, and set out on a journey into the unknown. No problem, right? But Abram knew God had a plan and there was something great out there that honored Him, so he gave the order and his family followed him. Opportunity knocked and security went out the window. Becoming Abraham meant a huge paradigm shift for the father of God's chosen people – new name, new location and a new life.

The Lord said to Abram, "Leave your native country, your relatives, and your father's family, and go to the land that I will show you. I will make you into a great nation. I will bless you and make you famous, and you will be a blessing to others."

Genesis 12: 1-2 (NLT)

And the same was true for Scott's church family. To realize the vision, all he had to do was give up his position as senior pastor, dissolve the church and merge with a different, larger church, turn an old supermarket into a church building, and move the congregation 15 miles to a new town. No problem, right? But Scott knew this supermarket building was a God-thing, so he never gave up on achieving the vision. Gaining greater impact in our region meant a huge paradigm shift for our church – new name, new location, and a new focus.

When Abram chose opportunity over security, the Hebrew nation arose, through which Jesus came.

When Scott Fetterolf chose opportunity over security, a church reached new levels of ministry. The supermarket-turned-church saw 2,003 people attend Christmas Eve gatherings. In that weekend alone, 131 acknowledged they'd visited for the very first time. Many have found a new life in Christ. Lives are changing. The mission is being fulfilled and the opportunity has become reality. And it all happened because one preacher led a congregation to choose opportunity when they were secure.

Now don't get me wrong. Giving up security doesn't mean being stupid. Set SMART goals. This concept is attributed to management guru, Peter Druker, and was first published by George Doran (Management Review, Vol. 70, Issue 11, pp. 35-36, 1981.) Good management goals should be:

S – Specific: Don't just plan to be better. Plan to be 70% better (or some specific goal you choose).
M – Measurable: You need a concrete measurement to assess your progress.
A – Attainable: Able to be accomplished with the available resources.
R – Relevant: The goal should address your overall mission and purpose.
T – Time-Based: Allow enough time for the plan to work and set a time to re-evaluate the plan.

Giving up security also doesn't mean success will happen in one brilliant explosion of faith. Be patient. God reminded Isaiah (55:8), "My thoughts are nothing like your thoughts…my ways are far beyond anything you could imagine." Adopt a marathon attitude. Multiple generations passed from Abram to Abraham until Jesus came to earth as a Jew. A total of 16 years spanned from Scott's arrival in Berwick to the first LCBC gathering in that supermarket church. Your opportunity will unfold as God sees fit.

What new opportunity to advance His mission is God showing you? What "impossible" dream are you bypassing in order to hang on to the things you know as safe and secure? The Bible records dozens of men and women who God handpicked to fulfill His mission on earth. And in every case, they met some sort of discomfort while striving to reach the goal. Will you be the next person God calls to choose opportunity over security?

TODAY'S CHALLENGE

1. **Eliminate Stinkin' Thinkin'**
   Is there an opportunity in your life that you are shrinking back from because it challenges your sense of security? Don't let that natural tendency to resist change just because it is hard hinder you. Others may be caught in that wrong thinking, too. As you choose opportunity over comfort there will be people who will tell you that you're crazy for giving up security. Get ready for the naysayers and stay focused.

2. **Initiate Awesome Actions**
   Listen to God as He speaks to you through His Word and in prayer, while accepting wise counsel from people who He places along your opportunity trail. After that analysis, if you feel He is leading, choose opportunity over security and go for it!

Chuck Humphrey

"Just keep blocking and tackling."

Scott was a mentor to many other pastors. Often times these pastors would ask what they could do to lead their church out of times of stagnation or to produce new excitement and growth. Scott would draw on his football coaching background to answer, "Just keep blocking and tackling." The Philly Special might have helped the Philadelphia Eagles win Super Bowl LII, but trick plays didn't get them into the Super Bowl. Consistent play week in and week out throughout the season made them champions. And since, to Scott, football was always a metaphor for life, if you get good at the basics, you'll succeed in church ministry, and the rest of life, too.

I know the first time I was the one asking how to jumpstart church growth I was disappointed with that answer. I was hoping there was some secret code that he had discovered that could unlock the secret to success. I thought that maybe in his vast experience he had developed some creative program or special event that would fire up the volunteers and generate excitement.

Lord knows there are plenty of church growth seminars to be taken. I've sat through some of them. Then I went back to church board meetings to hash out vision statements, mission statements, and five-year plans. During a series of meetings over a number of months, we listed all of our priorities and tried to make a cohesive mission statement (or was it a vision statement?). It ended up something like, "Our mission is to bring people to a saving knowledge of Christ in a challenging but inoffensive way and then provide effective discipleship programs for them and their families with appropriate age and maturity level curriculum, in a loving and inclusive environment, and provide a weekly worship experience that is authentic and God focused in a culturally relevant style, while also providing for people's physical and emotional needs and …" You get the point. It turned out that our five-year plan ended up being to finalize the mission statement (or so it seemed). My five-year plan was to get off church board.

If you really want a five-year plan, you can hire a church growth consultant and they'll give you a packet full of marketing ideas and have you doing team building exercises to accomplish success. But at the end of the day, after you've fallen backwards off a table and been caught by your team members, a fundamental truth lies in Scott's simple message.

Keep blocking.

Keep tackling.

To be an effective church, Scott encouraged us to focus on two things: First, providing a weekend experience where people could join for worship and receive a biblical message that was clear and applicable to their lives. And second, giving opportunities for people to learn how to live Christ-centered lives. If you execute these essential components well, people's lives will change, and those changed lives will impact other lives.

So, keep blocking and tackling.

We fail when we get pulled off our essential focus by adding lots of good things that drain our resources and distract us from the primary purpose of introducing people to Christ and helping them grow in that relationship. When the church loses its essential mission, it falters. And adding more fancy programs isn't the answer. It is time to get back to blocking and tackling.

This is not just a message for church leaders. If you have lost your way in life, go back to the basics. Discard the distractions that have led you astray. Rediscover the things that are essential and do them well. Then keep doing them. Success will follow.

In the first century, another seasoned church leader, John, one of the Jesus's disciples who became a leader in the early Church, was mentoring a group of Christians in Ephesus. He sent them a message when they had gotten off track. We don't know the specifics, but we can tell that they started strong and were doing well but somehow had gotten into a slump. Had they played football back then John undoubtedly would have told them to get back to focusing on blocking and tackling. Instead, he just told them to get back to doing the things they did at first. Get back to the fundamentals.

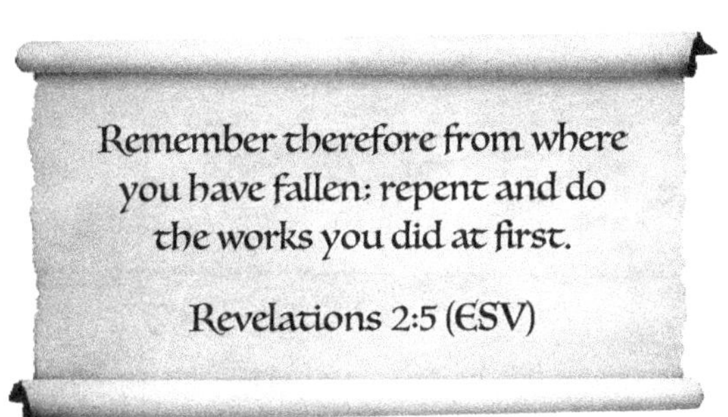

I went through a period of burnout in my life when I was leading a growing church, teaching robotic surgery around the country, and managing a busy surgical practice – all great things. I basically had three fulltime jobs. I was always tired, frustrated, and had growing anxiety. So, it was time for change. We joined a larger church and I stepped aside to let new staff run the church – who did a much better job than I ever could, I might add. I slashed my teaching schedule so I could spend less time in airports and more time at home. I left private practice and became employed by a local physician group to eliminate practice management headaches. I eliminated the things that were robbing my strength and keeping me from accomplishing my primary goal of treating patients. These were all big choices, but they were necessary to get me back to doing the essentials well.

I also focused on some health essentials. Instead of spending my evenings trying to catch the work details that were falling through the cracks, I started exercising, got better rest, and was eating real meals instead of plastic wrapped carry-on plane food. The results were dramatic. More focus. Less anxiety. A sense of margin in my life. All by getting back to blocking and tackling.

TODAY'S CHALLENGE

1. **Eliminate Stinkin' Thinkin'**
   Are you feeling like you are running from one activity to another but not accomplishing as much as you'd like? Is your spiritual life, family relationships, or your career struggling because you are stretched too thin? It is probably because of the wrong thinking that doing more is better. Resolve to do less things more effectively. Examine your life for things that may be good but are distracting you from accomplishing essential goals.

2. **Initiate Awesome Actions**
   If you have identified non-essential activities that are distracting you from the essentials, it is time to pull the plug on those things. Find things you spend time on that are draining your energy and making you less effective overall and stop them. Find things that you are wasting money on and cancel the subscription. Then, once you have regained some margin in life, protect it. When some new option arises in life, if it is not essential just say, "No."

Clark Gerhart

"Sometimes we all need a little jerk space."

Have you ever thought that there are people in your life who have the spiritual gift of being a jerk?

Maybe it's your annoying boss who is always demanding more from you. It could be your mother-in-law who never has a kind word to say to you. Or, perhaps it's your spouse after a long day (or before they've had their morning coffee), your kids, your rude neighbor, or the guy who just cut you off in traffic.

I don't know who it is for you, but chances are there is somebody in your life (probably multiple somebodies) who you would say can get under your skin and be a real jerk at times.

And guess what? You're right. No matter who it is that came to your mind, you're right, they certainly can be a jerk at times.

But you know what else? You and I can be real jerks sometimes, too.

Don't believe me? Let's take a quick inventory together. Think back to any time you have ever been in an argument with somebody. Have you ever taken a cheap shot at that other person in the heat of the moment? Said something that you knew would be hurtful? That was a jerk moment.

Have you ever told someone something to their face that was the opposite of what you said behind their back? Jerk moment.

Has anyone ever tried to talk to you, but you just weren't listening? Maybe you were checking your phone, focusing on your list of things to do that day, or not looking away from the television. Yep, that's a jerk moment, too.

Ever told someone you'd do something, knowing you wouldn't? Super jerk moment.

Every single one of us find ourselves in situations where that inner jerk comes out – ours or the other person's. Now, what if every time you or I had one of those jerk moments, we blew up our relationship over it? What if every jerk moment was allowed to make a permanent impact on our relationships?

If that was the case for me, I'm sure that I wouldn't even have anybody left in my life to be a jerk to – they would have ditched me a long time ago.

That's why *jerk space* is so important. Scott defined jerk space as, "the extra grace that we all need just for living and breathing as a human on Earth." Believe it or not, you don't have to tell them they're a jerk every time they act like one. You don't have to get upset. You don't have to hold it against them. You can give space, allowance for each other's faults, as Paul talked about in his letter to the Colossians.

> Make allowance for each other's faults and forgive anyone who offends you. Remember, the Lord forgave you, so you must forgive others.
>
> Colossians 3:13 (NLT)

I need jerk space from the people around me, as do you. And since we need to get jerk space *from* others, we need to choose to give jerk space *to* others.

Husbands (myself included), what if the next time your wife snapped at you after a stressful day at work, you maintained your cool and were above-and-beyond kind?

Wives, what if when your hubby forgot to do the dishes (after you asked for the 82nd time ... we're often a forgetful bunch) you didn't angrily remind him how lazy he is?

What if when your kid gives you lip, your boss gets overly critical, or the person in the check-out line makes a scene, you just said to yourself, "Well, that was a jerk moment. But I have those too, so I can give them the space to be a jerk and not get bent out of shape." Imagine how de-escalating and freeing that would be for your relationships!

Now, here's what I'm not saying. I'm not saying giving jerk space is the same as condoning what they did. I'm not saying you should never confront someone about what they did wrong. And I'm not saying you need to be best friends with every jerk around you. But, as Scott taught me, your relationships will have a lot more peace and happiness in the mix when giving jerk space is a regular part of what both parties do, rather than getting hung up on every potential conflict.

And yes, I understand that many of us have been hurt in some really big ways. It wasn't just a jerk space kind of thing. It was awful. It cut you deep to the core. It's not something that you can just let go. However, the same principle holds true: The longer you hold onto that pain and bitterness, the more you hurt yourself. So, when jerk space isn't enough, you might have to put in some work to get your heart right again. Whether that's through a hard conversation, counseling, lots of prayer, or even distancing yourself from that person, working to a place of forgiveness and healing is critical.

For those of us who are Christians, this is bigger than just a helpful way to have healthy and happy relationships, though it is that. It's a command from God. If we're Christians, we've been forgiven of much. We've been forgiven of more than we'll have to forgive of others. And, when we keep in mind that our entire rap sheet has been cleared, we can give some grace to those around us.

The next time someone is a jerk (not if, but when) you have a choice: You can either expect the person to be perfect and be shocked that they could ever do wrong. Or, you can recognize that we all can be jerks and just give them some space to be a jerk – the same jerk space that you and I need.

TODAY'S CHALLENGE

1. **Eliminate Stinkin' Thinkin'**
   If someone is a jerk to you, are you quicker to get offended or to let it go? Are you quick to forget the times that you have been a jerk? When tempted to focus only on other people's jerkiness, remind yourself that you can be a jerk sometimes, too. And remember that forgiving the jerks around you doesn't require condoning what they did or said. It just means giving them a little space to be jerks until they figure it out.

2. **Initiate Awesome Actions**
   Cultivate a habit of giving jerk space in the moment. Recognize jerk moments as they occur and choose to rise above them. The whole point to jerk space is that you don't have to respond to every jerkish comment. If you are really offended and you feel you have to express your feelings to the jerk, do it without being a jerk back. If they are a friend, they'll care, and fix the relationship. If they don't care, they may need not only jerk space, but some real space, too. Healthy boundaries are part of good relationships.

Brad Travelpiece

"There is nothing you can do to be more or less pleasing to God. Enjoy that."

If you're a Christian and I told you that you are completely forgiven and fully pleasing to God because of Christ and his redemption, and that there is nothing you can do to be more or less pleasing to God, you would probably say, "Yeah, sure. That's the whole point of Christianity, right?"

But now I want to ask you, "Do you enjoy that fact?"

Don't answer yet. Let me ask a few more questions.

Do you ever feel bad about yourself because you've screwed up? Do you ever feel dirty or ashamed or unworthy? Do you ever feel like you can't talk to God because of that thing – you know, *that* thing – that you do that you don't like to talk about? Do you feel like bad things that happen in life are God punishing you? If any of those answers are "yes" you're not enjoying it.

Or maybe you're the girl or guy that every pastor loves because you can't say "no" when asked to volunteer but you're starting to feel like a rubber band that's about to snap. Maybe you're the guy who always shows up to help their friends but feels like no one is ever around when you need a hand. Or perhaps you're the girl who sends monthly support to a child overseas, has automatic deposit for her weekly church donations, but is growing resentful that her budget always seems tight at the end of the month. If any of that sounds like you, then you're not enjoying it.

Christ's sacrifice has resolved our issues with God *once and for all,* as we see in Hebrews 10:10. Jesus paid the penalty, so we never have to feel like a convict. He paid the fine. He did the time. He took care of all the dumb, insensitive, hurtful, dirty, ugly things we have ever done and ever will do, once and for all. It is over. Or in Jesus' words from the cross, "It is finished." John 19:30.

And finished means *finished*! If you think there is something to add to what Christ already did, it will have to be better than living a sinless life and dying on a cross. You got better than that?

> Under this new plan we have been forgiven and made clean by Christ's dying for us once and for all.
>
> Hebrews 10:10 (TLB)

So, stop trying to make yourself look better and worrying about how bad you look. There is nothing you could do wrong to make Him love you less. Consider the prodigal son who screwed up royally and was still given a son's homecoming party. And, nothing you could do right to make Him love you more. Case in point, the prodigal son's big brother. He did everything right and thought he'd get some extra gold stars to put by his name on his homework assignment. The Father's response was, "That's awesome and you already get everything a son is entitled to!" You can't make it better. You can't make it worse. You literally could genuinely accept Christ's sacrifice for your sin and sit on the couch playing video games the rest of your life and you'd be loved by God as His child.

Ah, but right now you're picturing a 40-year-old kid, still in their parent's basement playing video games and you're saying that could never be a true representation of a Christian. Well, consider that the kid in the basement of their parent's house is still in the house. They may not be one of the parent's brightest stars, but they can never stop being the parent's kid. They may want better things for their child, sure. But their relationship was established with one inexorable event when that kid was born making them a son or daughter. It's the same with you. In one irrevocable moment you became reborn as God's son or daughter. And that can't change.

Enjoy that.

Don't get me wrong, confessing sin and growing in holiness and sanctification is a wonderful thing that occurs in our lives after we accept Christ. But don't fear it. He's not the angry slave driver. He's a loving Father guiding you, His child, into maturity. Making you better at every step. Enjoy it.

It's also true that ministry, service and generosity should all be part of the Christian life. But if it is drudgery to you, stop doing it! It's not scoring you points with God. Christ scored all the points you'll ever need. Do only those things that you can do out of a pure motive of appreciation for what God has done for you. And, enjoy it.

We have been made holy through the sacrifice made by Jesus Christ, once for all. When it becomes more than head knowledge and you really believe it, you will enjoy it.

TODAY'S CHALLENGE

1. **Eliminate Stinkin' Thinkin'**
   Re-ask yourself the questions above and really examine your feelings toward God. Do you think you would need to stop doing some bad things or start doing some more good things to make yourself more pleasing to God? If so, it is time to confront that thinking with the outrageous love of God that could never love you more or less because it is all based on His character not yours. When religious pride or condemnation try to convince you that you may be more or less pleasing to God, recognize the smell and stop the stinkin' thinkin' before it re-infects your mind.

2. **Initiate Awesome Actions**
   Examine some of the more important activities in your life. The ones outside of brushing your teeth and going to work every day. The ones that affect you spiritually. Getting sinful behavior out of your life is certainly a good thing. But while doing so, remember that you are already fully loved. Cleaning up your act is not about relieving guilt. It is about leading a healthier, less encumbered life that pleases your loving Father. You can enjoy that.

   Likewise, if you are doing good things but are growing resentful because they are not giving you the warm fuzzies that you had hoped, stop doing them. You're not gaining love-points with God. You don't need points with God. Do only those things that you can do out of sincere appreciation for the love you already have, and you can enjoy that a whole lot more.

Clark Gerhart

"Get over yourself. You're not that important."

Everybody is full of themselves these days. I'm just as guilty as the next guy. Social media is my vice. While it is an enormously useful tool to invite people to church, promote the Gospel and celebrate my family, I must admit that there are times when I'm convinced the whole world needs to know where I've been and what I've done.

Why?

Because I'm important! I have 1,407 friends on Facebook!

Scott Fetterolf was one of the few people I've ever met that truly knew he wasn't important. In fact, he was afraid too many people thought he was important.

Scott was hired by our church when it had just about imploded. He was sharp, edgy and impactful and lives were changing as a result. Under his leadership, the church grew exponentially. To say the church building was bursting at the seams sounds cliché, but we were literally moving walls to accommodate the growth.

But being the visionary he was, Scott was also unsettled. The success of the church and his ministry had a fatal flaw. He knew the church had no plan for *A.S.* (After Scott) and he feared there was way too much focus on one guy – Scott! He would often joke, "What if I get hit by a beer truck*?*"

So, the growth continued, but without a workable plan for what would come next. A new path forward was critically necessary. As the winds of change began blowing, I had the honor and weight of having to help adjust the sails and keep the ship afloat as a member of the church's elder board. So, I felt the storm coming first hand.

Then God opened a huge window of opportunity.

Lives Changed By Christ Church (LCBC), a multi-site church in Pennsylvania, showed interest in facilitating a merger between our two church families. Scott saw this church marriage as a huge "God thing," and he predicted it would become a mission force like our area had never before experienced. He feverishly championed the move despite the fact that his personal role would change drastically. He'd no longer be top dog. He'd teach less (at first not at all) and someone else would ultimately call the shots.

One night, following the meeting where we made the decision to recommend a churchwide referendum on pulling the trigger on the merger, Scott was quieter than normal. I pulled him aside and looked him in the eye and asked him point blank, "Are you okay with this?" I told him that I wouldn't cast my final vote unless I was certain that he would be okay post-merger.

He actually said, "No." But it wasn't an opposition "No," just an honest statement that he didn't want us to vote against change, even for his sake. Change was necessary and about to happen.

He went on to explain, "Look, this isn't about me. It's about the mission. And I'll be okay."

Continually, throughout the merger decision process, he reminded us that advancing the mission would be uncomfortable. This was Scott's uncomfortable, but it was clear that gaining firepower for God was all that mattered to him even if change felt uncertain in that moment.

I knew he was right.

That night reinforced a valuable truth for me: It's never about me. It's always about Jesus and pointing others to Him. The mission of the Gospel can only advance when our eyes are on Him.

Many times since, I've reflected on that night because it lit a fire inside of me, shining light on my own shortcoming. Painfully I realized that for many years I was engrossed in what I was doing for the church instead of reflecting what Jesus did for me on the cross.

Over time it hit me that from being a young boy, growing up in the church through adulthood, most of what I thought was service was really performance. It was more about who Chuck was in relation to the church – who saw *me* and what *I* did – instead of who saw *Jesus* and what *He* did.

If anyone could say he was important to the mission it was John the Baptist. He was a famous preacher who drew large crowds and was impacting his region. And yet John 3:30 tells us when Christ showed up John made clear that he wasn't that important. Christ is the One who came to save the world.

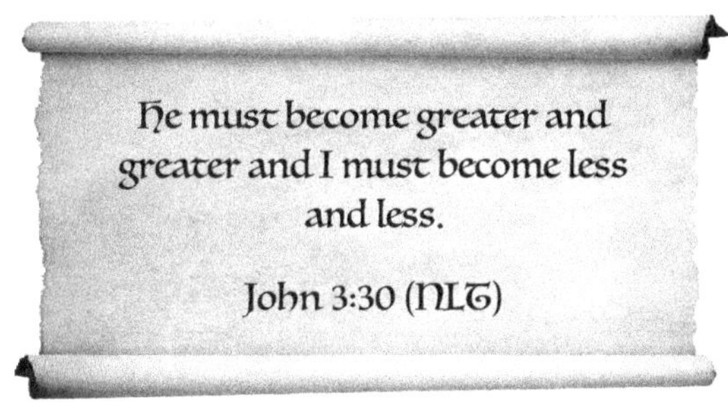

When we choose to focus on becoming more like Jesus we all enroll in a college course called "getting over ourselves" and we learn that all of our life accomplishments pale in the light of His sacrifice. Compared to Jesus, we are not that important.

Scott earned a master's degree in getting over himself, setting a life example for all of us. Me, I'm still working on that degree daily as God continually shows me more and more that I'm definitely not that important!

How about you? Are you studying for your degree?

TODAY'S CHALLENGE

1. **Eliminate Stinkin' Thinkin'**
   When you are offended, frustrated or feeling critical in church ask yourself, "Am I making this about me instead of the mission?" Remember that ultimately it is not about you and me. You or me being in charge or getting the credit isn't the goal. It doesn't matter if we like the color of the curtains or the songs being sung. This is not about spreading the good news about us. If someone else's leadership, the décor or the music are drawing people to the Good News of the Savior of the World it should be fine with us. When we make our own priorities the goal, we almost always weaken the impact of God's greater mission.

2. **Initiate Awesome Actions**
   To make your actions awesome emphasize humility. Start by praying daily for God to show you each and every time you are so full of yourself that you fail to advance Christ's mission. (This is a dangerous prayer. Be prepared to be completely humbled!) When you are given the opportunity to lead, demonstrate humility by pushing others forward and avoiding self-promotion. See your work in ministry as service, not for personal gain. Practice humility by doing something for others that costs you something. For example: Give away your reputation to stand with someone who is being bullied … give time serving at church … give up money by prioritizing your family and times of service over work.

Chuck Humphrey

"Ministry is messy. Lean in and embrace the mess."

You may think that in this day of modern technology that treating patients is pretty much by the numbers. Do some blood work, get a CT scan and then zap the problem with a laser. If only it was that straight forward! So, so, so (I might need a few more "so's" actually) many other factors influence medical decisions, making it rarely that simple.

Some patients refuse treatment out of fear. Others reject medical recommendations and opt for "cures" they read about on the internet. Most patients have unhealthy behaviors and addictions that complicate their treatment. Occasionally, the very best treatment isn't covered by a patient's insurance. That's a tough one. Sometimes it's social issues like, "I know I have cancer, Doc, but I have to wait on chemo until my granddaughter gets married this Fall." One of the most difficult is the estranged child who shows up after decades without contact and wants to control the medical decisions for their elderly parent instead of the local sibling. That one's an emotional mine field. You'd think medical care would be all sterile and calculated. But it's not. It's messy.

It is just as true when caring for people spiritually. "Ministry is Messy," is a mantra that has circulated in Christian circles the last few years. It is tough to pin it on one person. It did not originate with Scott, but he used it to help his staff and volunteers have realistic expectations about what ministry would look and feel like.

I have found that physical care in medicine, and spiritual care in church, are really very similar. They both tend to be messy because both involve humans. And humans are messed up by their sinful natures.

The bottom line: Ministry is messy because humans are messy.

Having accepted that, you have two choices. You can pull back from the mess or you can lean in. Scott always encouraged us to lean in.

It's tempting to pull back when the mess gets really messy. You may be shocked to think any Christian would actually pull back from helping people in need, but we do. We will drop our used clothes in the drop-off bin for the homeless, but what if one shows up at church smelling like he lives in a sewer – mostly because he lives in a sewer. Do you give him the bum's rush out the door to protect the church's potpourri atmosphere? How about the single Mom who creates too much of a commotion corralling her unruly kids and interrupts your Christian worship experience. Would you have her and her pack of miscreants ushered out of the auditorium? Would you feel uncomfortable if a member of the LGBT visited your church? Do you feign off the invitation to join coworkers at a bar after work citing a scheduling conflict to avoid being seen where people who drink alcohol hang out? Do you hang out with *any* friends outside of church or do you only socialize with nice healthy – un-messy – Christians? If these are true of you – as they all too often have been true of me in the past – you may be avoiding the mess because it's too messy.

Other times we avoid the mess because we have been-there-and-done-that and had the life sucked out of us by messy people who wouldn't – or couldn't – change. That person who falls off the wagon and lands in your lap when they start drinking for the 300th time. The person who calls you every Friday night when another dating relationship goes off the tracks. It's easy to run from those messes.

There certainly are benefits to avoiding the mess – like not getting blood sprayed on you – but if cleanliness drives you there will be no opportunity to cut open a trauma victim's chest and reach in and grab the pulmonary artery before they bleed out! That's a patient whose life you really change, not the one sitting around drinking kale smoothies and being healthy. Hanging out with Christians and talking about how great it is to be saved would be the same. No snatching people from the jaws of damnation. No seeing wrecked lives become new. To see those victories you have to lean in and grab hold of lives that are bleeding out spiritually: the sick, the broken, the messed up. The ones who make it messy.

The key is balance between calling out people when their behaviors are destructive and need to change, and extending grace when people need patience and time to process and heal. Zechariah talks about this balance, telling us that God compels us to both judge fairly *and* show mercy and kindness. If you never call out bad behavior, a person will never have the opportunity to repent and change. But don't forget that all important little word *and* in between. It's judging right from wrong *and* being merciful and kind, recognizing that there is always a back story to why people's lives are so messy, and that we all have shortcomings and need grace. Sometimes you draw clear boundaries and hold people accountable. Sometimes you choose to be patient with a person's mess, while you kindly help them deal with deeper issues.

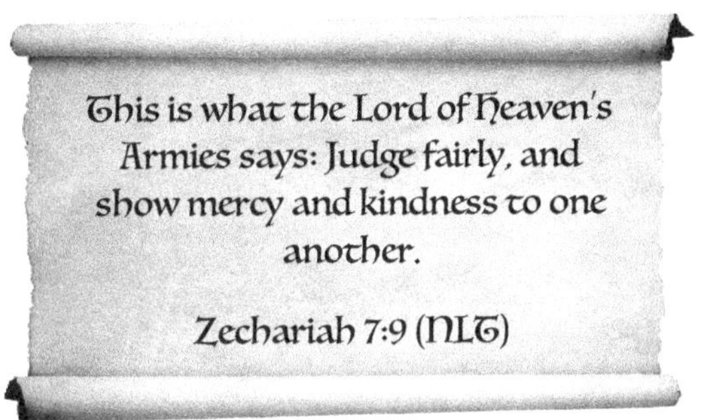

Success is in the balance and the fulcrum on which the balance pivots is discernment, which tells you when the balance is tipping too far in one direction. You may tend to avoid the mess by standing off in judgement. Or, you may feel overwhelmed by the mess and want to run the other way. When it seems too messy, discern whether you need more fair judgment or more mercy and kindness. Then, lean in and address the mess head on.

TODAY'S CHALLENGE

1. **Eliminate Stinkin' Thinkin'**
   Have you avoided or backed away from Christian ministry? If so, think about why. Is dealing with people that are messy unappealing? Or, have you been down the road and around the corner with messy people and come away drained and feeling used? Think about which direction you tend to tip that balance when the mess becomes too messy. Are you prone to standing back and casting judgment, holding people accountable for their destructive behaviors without grace? Or, do you tend to extend mercy to all, letting people stay stuck in repetitive, destructive behaviors and giving yourself away over and over until you have nothing left to give? Recognize the need for balance.

2. **Initiate Awesome Actions**
   If you tend to avoid the mess by standing off in judgment, identify that person or types of people you most often criticize or condemn. Find time to talk with them, get to know their back story, and explore the struggles they face in life that produce some of the mess.

   If you run from the mess because it has sucked the life out of you, identify that person or types of people who tend to drain you of time, energy and/or money. Set up some real boundaries. Find resources outside of yourself that can help meet their needs.

   Address the reason that makes you avoid the mess and then lean in!

Clark Gerhart

"I don't take my theology lightly, but I don't hold on to it too tightly."

In high school I wanted to develop my faith and grow in maturity. I thought that meant getting smarter, so I studied theology. I read about how Paul would teach and preach in synagogues and Gentile lecture halls. To me that seemed like a good way to flesh out the finer details of what I was studying. But I didn't have a synagogue or a lecture hall, so naturally, I went to the basketball court. One of those times, playing a pick-up game, and having a casual theological conversation with a friend, he asked me, "So, are you Armenian or Calvinist?" I didn't know what that meant, so I played it off and looked it up later. A lot of what Calvin taught sounded ludicrous to me, so I went to Dad (Scott Fetterolf) to figure out how to refute it. He paused, grinned at me, and said, "Well, actually, I believe that, Seth." I was shocked and angry, so I didn't really respond. Fortunately, that night was haircut night, so I had an out and I stalked off.

A little while later I was sitting in our bathroom while mom worked intently with the clippers. Dad walked down the hall and sat on the floor facing me. We had a long conversation about the question I had asked him. True to form, he didn't give me any answers but helped me navigate through what I was thinking and feeling and pointed me in a good direction to develop a conviction of my own. At the end of the conversation he said, "I don't take my theology lightly, but I don't hold on to it too tightly."

It's one of my favorite memories with him.

A quick Google search will tell you that theology is "the study of religious faith, practice, and experience; especially the study of God and of God's relation to the world." The first half of that definition makes me gag. Isn't that what it has often become though? Just a bunch of facts and beliefs? But even Google recognizes the root of theology: The study of God. What a beautiful idea! What if theology lived up to its original intent? To *know* God. Not just to know about God. Not apologetics of unprovable, intangible ideas. Not definitive proclamations on the meaning of prophecy. Tribulations. Dispensations. Camps of thought named after men. All of these can be positive avenues to know about God, but they're not the substance. I wouldn't spend too much time there.

That's the essence of what my dad was saying. Be thoughtful and intentional about how you develop your understanding of "religious faith, practice, and experience" but don't hold on to it too tightly. It'll change as you grow. What really matters is your day-to-day knowing of God, who He is, who He's made you, and how you should therefore live.

What does it take to really *know* someone? God gave us a picture of this, and He didn't use a fact sheet or a stat line. He used sex. As in, "Adam *knew* Eve and she conceived and bore Cain." (Genesis 4:1) While a systematic repetition of your religious denomination's doctrines isn't useless, it *is* shallow. You can do that without really knowing the God behind the doctrines. It would be like spending your whole married life describing your wife's body without actually taking her to bed … to know her … biblically.

On the other hand, if you go beyond the Bible stories and describe the compassion Jesus had as He healed a leper, or the mercy he felt for the woman caught in adultery who he saved from stoning … or even greater, empathize with him in those … you'd be getting to really know his heart. That's what He's looking for from his bride, the Church, you and me. He wants us to know Him, not just know about Him.

Jesus addressed this idea in John 5. He had just been accused of breaking the Law by healing a man on the Sabbath. His explanation to the theologians of the day is pointed and challenging. Full of love and ferocity. Jesus says to them, you're looking for life in the Law itself, in your interpretation and execution of it. But all of that points to me! I AM LIFE! But you won't come to me! You're lost in the ideas. I am the substance.

Titus 3:5 says that Jesus died for us so that he could bring us to God. Don't make the same mistake as the Pharisees by trying to come by another way. Release a tight grip on theological ideas and take hold of the Son of God. Pour your passion into knowing God as revealed through Jesus. Meditate on the things that He taught and imitate the things that He did.

In one of His last prayers on Earth Jesus said He had made Himself known to His disciples, and He would continue to do that. He wants to be known by us! He wants to share His thoughts and His heart with us in every situation we find ourselves. That's the true *knowing*. How cool is that?

TODAY'S CHALLENGE

1. **Eliminate Stinkin' Thinkin'**
   Do you like to debate religious ideas? Have you ever lost a friend over a theological argument? Do you feel zeal for pointing out other's impurities, or do you have compassion for other's brokenness? Are you quicker to throw stones or extend mercy? There are doctrines that we have to hold very tightly, but I'm pretty sure the list is small. Consider where you might be holding to doctrine too tightly at the expense of knowing God's heart.

2. **Initiate Awesome Actions**
   If any of the above questions hit home with you, maybe it is time to spend less time knowing *about God* and more time knowing *Him*. Get to know Jesus by reading through one of the Gospels every month for the next year. That'll get you through each one three times. Ask God to imprint the character of Jesus on your heart until it spills out of you.

Seth Fetterolf

"When God says we are a new creation, we actually believe it."

At a church leadership meeting, Scott and the group were discussing a policy that excluded divorced people from being involved in ministry. I was not at this meeting, but I have been at many like it and the discussion usually ranges along similar lines. Some people emphasize the Bible passages that explain the importance of marriage and the prohibitions towards divorce. Others stress the need for Christians to represent Christ's character to the world. Still others point out the reality that divorce is so common in society that we must accept it to be culturally relevant.

At this particular meeting, I am told, that after some discussion someone turned to Scott and asked, "How have you dealt with this in the churches you pastored?" And … in typical straight-to-the-point Scott fashion … he replied, "Well, when God says we are a new creation we actually believe it."

Yikes, you mean people with one type of sin that is covered by Christ can be in ministry alongside all sorts of other sinners whose sins are likewise covered by Christ? It's so simple it might just work.

Now, don't get me wrong, there are ramifications to being involved in ministry, especially leadership, and I don't want you to think these are easy issues for churches. In fact, I don't want to debate church policies here at all. But I do want to ask you this: How would it affect you if you *actually* believed that when you repent of your sin … no matter what type of sin … and accept Christ that you become a new creation? Not just a forgiven, old, worn out sinner, but genuinely forgiven and made into a new and improved version of yourself … and the *past* really has *passed*, as in today's verse.

The difficulty here is that we do not look different on the outside. It would be nice if we developed a glowing cross on our foreheads like the Christians in the *Left Behind* book series by Tim LaHaye and Jerry B. Jenkins (Tyndale House Publishers). It would be easy to know who is really saved and who isn't. But we don't get a visible sign in our outward appearance. We do not always see a dramatic change in our outward behavior right way, either. So, it can be tough to accept the idea that a transformation has taken place. But God promises that we are transformed into something new.

Gene Edwards helps us understand this transformation in his book *The Divine Romance* (Tyndale House Publishers, Inc., 1993) and why becoming a new creation is essential. He starts by reviewing the *old* creation. God makes the world and a bunch of animals. That's just OK. He needs something more. So, He makes Adam. Still not right, there's only one of him. So, God makes Eve. Now it's getting good. The cool part about Eve is that God started with one of Adam's ribs, so she was literally made of the same stuff as Adam. Now creation is good. Everyone has a mate. Humans had other humans…. animals other animals. Perfect.

Well, not quite perfect. It was only good. Because God had no companion with His divine nature. So, God devised a way to fix that. He'd make a *new creature*. He would take a part of Himself and place it into men and women, transforming them, making them something new. Just like Eve was to Adam, they would be made of the same stuff He was, and at last God would have a companion of His same species. At least in Edwards' allegorical view.

Putting allegory aside, let's re-enter the real world. We have been told Bible stories since we were kids, so we think becoming a new creature is just another children's story. But what if it is not just a spiritual metaphor. What if, in some way that we cannot fully understand, when we accept Christ, we don't only get forgiven, Christ indwells us … like we say He does … and that God substance within us transforms us into a new creation?

What if we actually believed that … that we are a new creature, just as 2 Corinthians 5:17 says?

Would we ever say that one of God's transformed followers was not worthy of serving Him? Would we ever feel dirty and despised? Would we ever shy away from those we perceive as stronger or more valuable? Would we shrink back from an opportunity God provided us because we felt inadequate? No! Because we are no longer who we were before Christ entered our life. We contain God stuff. And God stuff is awesome. Therefore, we are awesome.

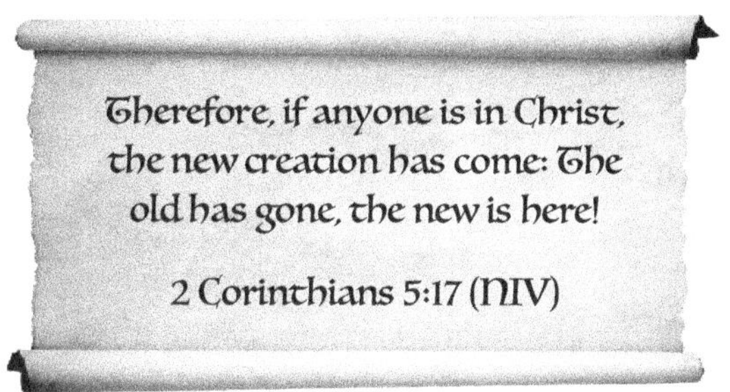

Now, just in case you were hoping to become god-like and take your god-ish new self out for a spin and create a new world or go ride an asteroid or something, that's not what this is about. Keep reading in 2 Corinthians 5:18-20. "God, who reconciled us to himself through Christ and gave us the ministry of reconciliation … We are therefore Christ's ambassadors, as though God were making his appeal through us." God made us into new creations so that we would become His ambassadors in this world, helping Him proclaim His message of reconciliation. So, no world of your own. Your job and mine is to transform this one.

So, be encouraged! You and the other transformed people with Jesus's God stuff inside them are new creatures with a big mission. Live in that confidence and proclaim the message of reconciliation to all who need to hear how deeply God loves them, forgives them, and wants to make them new.

And, if we do that during our time in this world, maybe in the next we get to ride asteroids. Who knows?

TODAY'S CHALLENGE

1. **Eliminate Stinkin' Thinkin'**
   Do you really (I mean *really*) believe that 2 Corinthians 5:17 means you are a new creature? I get that we may not totally understand how it happens, but do you *believe* it? That means thoughts of condemnation and guilt after you've been made new, are just stinkin' thinkin' that need to be eliminated.

2. **Initiate Awesome Actions**
   You can no longer see yourself as just an animal scurrying around this earth trying to eat and breed. You are a new creation. You have God-stuff inside you and a new assignment to become God's ambassador to this world. That should change the way you approach each new day. See your daily interactions with others as representing God's love for mankind and His desire to reunite His people with Himself. Look for ways to fulfill your new role as Christ's ambassador to this world.

Clark Gerhart

"Keep your head where your feet are."

In the song *What Ifs,* Kane Brown and Lauren Alaina struggle to decide whether their relationship is right or not. Kane repeats Lauren's concerns back to her, "You say what if I hurt you, what if I leave you. What if I find somebody else and I don't need you?" But, he turns it around and asks her to consider another possibility, "What if I was made for you, and you were made for me? What if this is it, what if it's meant to be?" What if? What if? What if?

I don't know how Kane and Lauren ended up. But I do know that getting caught up in "what ifs" will make you lose sight of what is happening right now. We worry about so many bad things that *could* happen and miss the good things that actually *are* happening.

A counselor calls it *predicting a negative future* and it is one of the trademarks of anxiety. To beat it, practice predicting a *positive* future by reminding yourself that there are plenty of positive "what ifs" in the future, too. In fact, you are more likely to find those positive outcomes if you keep your head focused on the realities of your situation … or as Scott would say, "Keep your head where your feet are."

What ifs can sneak up on you and punch you in the face with discouragement. A few months after I left a good job to enter an internship in Christian ministry, I found out that the company I left was giving out $1,000 bonuses in response to President Trump's tax reform law in 2017. In a family text-feed I ranted, "What the heck? Right when I leave?!" followed by a "Grrrr" and a really angry looking emoji. I was pretty pissed. In my head I was questioning that my feet might have been better off at my old job. My dad typed back Scott's quote, which he knew I had already heard from him, "Keep your head where your feet are." And I can tell you, my feet (and the rest of me) were never happier than when working in ministry. I found way more value in my life at my new position, than that $1,000 would ever have bought me.

I also know focusing on the fantasy you wish your life was, is not beneficial and just leads to heartache, resentment, bitterness, and a "woe is me" mentality. You are not a victim from life or the cards that were dealt to you. In Christ, you are a victory in process. You may not have arrived at the victory yet, but if you are always focusing on what you *don't* have, you will never be able to appreciate what you *do* have.

We've got to make the most of what we do have today by living wisely, as it says in Ephesians. It's not wisdom that leads many working moms and dads to think about work when their feet are at home, and then have their minds on home when their feet were at work. Having your head and feet in different places is a frustrating way to live. I have known people who thought their feet should be in the ritzy corner office instead of the mundane cubicle where they currently sit. But if you haven't gone through the process to perfect your skills and gain the knowledge needed for the boss's job, then you're not ready for advancement. So, keep your head where your feet are and focus on doing the very best where you're at.

> So be careful how you live. Don't live like fools, but like those who are wise. Make the most of every opportunity in these evil days.
>
> Ephesians 5:15-16 (NLT)

Ever get senioritis before graduating? Your head has already graduated but you still have classes to pass under your feet. You may be able to survive it in your last semester, but when your head checks out as a sophomore, you are definitely not making summa cum laude.

It's also not wise to let our minds be pulled into past pains. That only brings that old negativity into the present. You've dated some losers before and wonder, "What if this guy turns out to be a jerk?" Well, most guys will be jerks once in a while, but honestly, so will you. If he is showing strong character traits now, don't let your head be pulled back into the past by "what ifs." Learn from past experiences, but don't let the past paralyze you.

Where your feet are now can be different and better, but it won't be unless you are careful to keep your head in the present and act wisely now. So, keep your head where your feet are.

TODAY'S CHALLENGE

1. **Eliminate Stinkin' Thinkin'**
   Is there a situation that has you paralyzed by "what ifs", or are you constantly predicting a negative future? Then, you're thinkin' – actually you are *expecting* – that God is going to let you down. Sure, bad things happen to all of us sometimes, but do you really think He's going to just let you crash and burn? If so, when worry threatens to bring you down, remember that God loves you like a father (Matthew 7:9-11) and has good things in store for you (Romans 8:28). Stand on those truths. Trust Him and turn those thoughts all the way around. Next time you are expecting the worst, imagine what the future would look like if things went well. Then you can think, "What if something great happens?!"

2. **Initiate Awesome Actions**
   Your *what if* sensor is going to alert you to possible danger ahead. That's good! The trick is to not let those emotions control you. Start by dumping all of your feelings on God – even the ones that say you feel like He'll let you down and life will fall apart – He's a big boy and can handle it. Once those feelings are out, be deliberate to examine the facts about the situation, Scriptural wisdom, and guidance from people you trust. Write them out. Then pray, listen, and wait. Through this process you have turned off the *what if* noise and you can hear Him when He answers.

Chelsea D'Albero

"Following Jesus is not so much about one big choice, but thousands of smaller ones."

As a young person our family vacations included a lot of Christian festivals and retreats. That meant a lot of meetings listening to evangelists. Some good. Some not so good. But nearly all of them ending the same way:

The altar call.

It was the time when everyone was challenged to get up out of our seat and go down front to declare our desire to change the way we were living. Or, on other nights, the challenge was to make the really big change and accept salvation. What pressure! I often wrestled internally. *Do I go down and say I'll make a change? Is this God talking to me or pressure the speaker is laying on me? If I stay seated will people look at me like I'm a lost soul, too bound in sin to get up and start a new life? Ugh.*

Now, this could just be my wounded inner child talking, who was dragged to too many church services, but I don't think so. Chances are, if you have grown up as a Christian, you have sat through one of those services. And your parents didn't even let you bring your Gameboy. *Shoot! Maybe it is my inner child crying out!*

The problem with these and so many other pressure-filled religious experiences, is that they assume change happens in an instant … with one step in the right direction … preferably down an aisle.

But human experience tells us that change happens one small step at a time. No ten-year-old boy ever stood by the bed of his father who was dying of cirrhosis and said, "I hope I can become an alcoholic and die in middle age with a bloated abdomen and yellow skin, leaving my family to fend for themselves." No little girl turns off a Cinderella movie and decides, "I don't want to find a guy who loves me and live happily ever after. I'd rather have one broken relationship after another and raise kids with dads they don't know, all by myself." No one sets a life goal of committing increasingly more serious crimes, bouncing in and out of jail over the years, until finally they land in a cell that will be their home until they die. And yet people end up in those scenarios all the time. One step at a time.

Lasting positive change happens in steps as well. The classic academic track goes like this: high school … college … grad school … job. Careers in business, the trades and artistic fields also have steps you must choose to reach success. Avoiding obesity requires a choice every time you eat. Getting in shape … *groan* … requires the hard (at least for me) and repetitive choice of moving your sluggish bod to the elliptical instead of the couch.

So, if nearly all of human experience requires multiple, small steps to reach a goal, why would we think spiritual progress can be made in an instant? In today's passage, Job said that God calls to us, His creation, to return to Him. But that reunion doesn't happen in one huge leap. "For now," he says, it is just one step at a time.

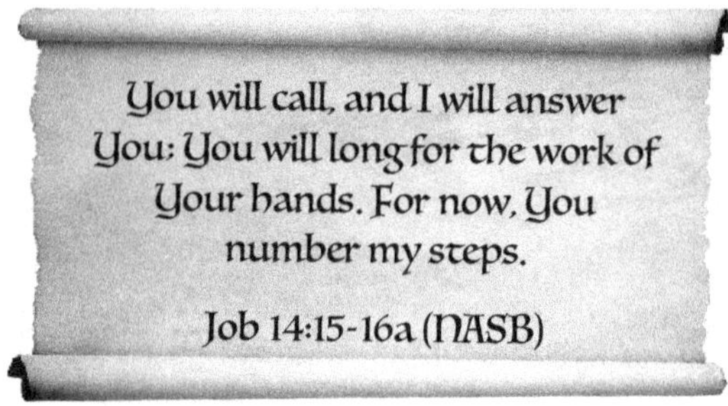

Don't get me wrong, effective speakers will challenge their listeners to act on what they are hearing. Some people have experienced deep, heartfelt change responding to the evangelist's challenge, but I believe even those dramatic events are the result of choices that prepared them for change. They chose to attend the meeting, after all!

So, salvation occurs after a series of choices leads you to a place of decision. That decision might happen in a church service, or it might happen while staring at the ceiling on a sleepless night when you finally give up and say, "God I need your help." Or maybe it happens as your spouse packs your kids in the car and you watch everyone who has ever loved you drive out the driveway, and your heart cries out, "God I need to learn how to love." Maybe it is when you look into a microscope or up at the stars and say, "This just couldn't happen by chance. God, I want to know who you really are." A series of steps leads to the moment when the spark of faith ignites, salvation occurs, and a life walking many more steps with God begins.

James Engel developed this idea in his book *What's Gone Wrong with the Harvest* (Zondervan, June 24, 1975), where he defined the emotional and intellectual choices that a person must make to go from not believing there is a god to fully following Christ. They are defined in the Engel Scale:

-10 No God framework
-9 Experience of emptiness
-8 Vague awareness of Christianity
-7 Interest in Christianity
-6 Awareness of the Gospel
-5 Positive attitudes to the Gospel
-4 Experience of Christian love
-3 Aware of personal need
-2 Grasp of implications of the Gospel
-1 Challenge to respond personally
0 Repentance and Faith
+1 Evaluation of the decision
+2 Learning the basics of the Christian life
+3 Functioning member of local church
+4 Continuing growth in character, lifestyle and service
+5 Effective sharing of faith and life

Here is why this is so important: If we see salvation as only occurring when we reach some designated end point, we – with *me* being the worst of *we* – see the world as containing the *saved* and the *unsaved*. The *us* and the *them*. Those *inside* the church and those *outside* the church. Scott cured me of this. His teaching was so impactful because he never spoke down from the pulpit to an audience of sinners. We are all the work of God's hands and He longs to have all of us return to Him. There was no *us* or *them* … no *insiders* or *outsiders*. Scott gave insights that he thought would help all of us take the next step on our spiritual journey in an atmosphere of love and acceptance. We should too. No need for pressure. We just encourage the other members of God's creation around us as we all continue walking closer with God.

TODAY'S CHALLENGE

1. **Eliminate Stinkin' Thinkin'**
   Do you often think of people around you as being either saved or unsaved? Us or them? If so, that thinking may be building walls between you and others. Try seeing everyone as somewhere along the same path back to God that you are following and see how doors open between you and other people along the journey.

2. **Initiate Awesome Actions**
   Use the Engel Scale in your next spiritual discussion with a friend or in a church group. Have people identify where they think they are on the scale. It will help them better understand their own beliefs and help you understand how to help them choose to take the next step.

Clark Gerhart

"Love God. Love others. It's not an option. It's a no-matter-what."

I don't think anyone would say the world at large is a particularly loving place. Lately, however, society is more of a battle field than a community. Our schools have literally become battlefields where armed officers patrol the halls ready to gun down weapon-wielding students before they commit mass murder. Our politicians gun down each other with personal attacks and partisan slurs, forcing wedges instead of fostering oneness. And, religious fanaticism drives people to all sorts of violence all around the globe.

Even in the smaller world where each of us live every day, there is no lack of people who make the world a worse place just by being in it. Their level of unlovability might be less than that of, say, a terrorist, but they can terrorize you nonetheless. They look pretty good on the outside, but when their feathers get ruffled they are pushy, demeaning, abrasive, angry, hurtful … just plain mean. It is really easy to let dislike – even hate – creep into your thoughts and your responses towards them.

I encountered one while working in the church office. He was a young husband and father who really seemed like he had it all together in public. But at home was mentally and emotionally abusing his wife. Pastor Scott was counseling this couple through a very hard session one day when the husband just unloaded on his wife. Scott brought the wife out to sit with me so he could have time with the husband. I talked with her a little, but mostly I just hugged her while she cried. I saw the pain on her face … the tears of hurt roll down her cheek. When the inner door opened I had nothing that I would call "loving thoughts" for the guy as he gathered up his wife to leave.

A few minutes later Scott came out of his office. Through moist eyes we looked at each other. This unpleasant interaction left us both very sad and a bit frustrated. There really was not much to say. As if to answer my unspoken question about how to help a person whose anger hurts people, Scott simply said, "Love God. Love others. It's not an option. It's a *no matter what.*"

It seemed like it was as much a reminder for himself as for me. It's a hard principle to apply. No matter what a person does, no matter how awful we feel they are, the answer is love.

This is not just *an important* Christian doctrine. It is *the most important.* Well, actually the *second* most important. But it is closely related to the first. When Jesus was asked what the most important commandment is, he said, "Love the Lord your God with all your heart and with all your soul and with all your mind and with all your strength. The second is this: Love your neighbor as yourself. There is no commandment greater than these."

> "Of all the commandments, which is the most important?" "The most important one," answered Jesus, "is this: 'Hear, O Israel: The Lord our God, the Lord is one. Love the Lord your God with all your heart and with all your soul and with all your mind and with all your strength.' The second is this: 'Love your neighbor as yourself.' There is no commandment greater than these."
>
> Mark 12:28-31 (NIV)

I'm not great at memorizing. I have a lot of Scripture buried in my heart, but I can't always get verses to pop back into my mind word-for-word when I need them. However, I can remember Scott's profound message to me that day. When the people around you are acting like jerks there is only one option: Love God and love others. I keep this Scriptural truth handy in the front of my mind because there are a lot of people who are difficult to love in this world, and I find myself saying it often.

If you are having trouble expressing love to someone, Gary Chapman tells us there are 5 ways people express and receive love in his book *The Five Love Languages* (Northfield Publishing, 1992). They are all good ways to express love, but everyone has one or two favorites out of the list that are the most effective ways to make them feel loved.

If you really want to express love to someone, use *their* love language not *yours*, Chapman suggests, or it may get lost in translation. The classic example is the grown child who tells their father, "You never loved me." To which he responds, "But I gave you everything!" He was a gift-giver and expressed his love by providing good things for his child. The child had a different love language, so he might as well have been speaking a foreign language. The love was never communicated in a way the child could feel.

Chapman's list is below with some of my suggestions for how to use them with those hard-to-love people:

1. Gift giving –a simple cup of coffee can melt a hard heart.
2. Quality time – spend time getting to know a person and you might discover the struggles they face that make them hard to love.
3. Words of affirmation – a kind word will usually diffuse hostility.
4. Acts of service – a helping hand can relieve the burdens that make people react to others out of stress.
5. Physical touch – a simple hand on the arm or shoulder can open doors to communication.

There are many profound and complex spiritual messages to guide us in the Christian life. Of all of them, this one has been my greatest help when I get angry with something happening in our world or I deal with someone difficult. Let it be the most important commandment for you, too. When you don't know how to respond. When you start to think poorly of someone. When you are tempted to return hate for hate, anger for anger, the answer is: “Love God. Love others. It’s not an option. It’s a no-matter-what.”

TODAY'S CHALLENGE

1. **Eliminate Stinkin’ Thinkin’**
   Does your spiritual life involve spending a lot of energy thinking about or even arguing deep theological issues? That isn’t really stinky stuff. It’s valuable. But it misses the mark compared to what Christ said was most important. Change your emphasis to pondering how to better love God and others.

2. **Initiate Awesome Actions**
   Find a person who needs to feel loved … it might even be that person that’s really hard to love. Pick the love language that *they* like best and show love to them. If you don’t know their love language, pick one. They’re all good!

Colleen Travelpiece

"Your plan 'B' is often God's plan 'A'. Roll with it."

When I left training my plan "A" was to have a job in a nice, small town, have a thriving career, become part of a community, and after 40 years or so, retire. For a few years it seemed like that might happen, until the small town where I was working turned out to not be such a nice place to work, for a whole bunch of reasons. I had to look for plan "B." Then one day, in the midst of really struggling with the should-I-stay-or-should-I-go dilemma, someone from a nearby, larger town asked me if I would come work with them. Wow. What timing. My plan "A" was falling apart. I wouldn't get the long stable career in one place that I had envisioned for myself. So, when a window opened, I leaped through it head first into plan "B".

As it turned out, my plan "B," turned out to be God's plan "A." The new organization had a much better work environment and more professional opportunities than I could have imagined back in my plan "A" job. That's because my plan "B" turned out to be God's plan "A". And, God's plan "A" was better than my plan "A".

Now, don't get me wrong, plan "B" doesn't always turn out to be awesome. It'd be nice if every time your plan "A" candy bar ends up a loser, the next day someone gives you a candy bar with a golden ticket and you win a free chocolate factory. But we all know that happens mostly in children's stories. In real life, plan "B's" can be a real bummer for a long time before the winning ticket shows up.

That is the way it was for Joseph. Plan "A" was to live happily ever after as Daddy's favorite child with lots of big brothers who would watch his back in a dangerous world. But at age 17 plan "B" came along when his brothers became the dangerous part of his dangerous world. They got tired of their spoiled little brother and locked him in a hole. Then, they sold him as a slave to a caravan hauling a load of goods down the highway to Egypt … who then handed him over to a rich guy named Potiphar … who handed him over to jail. Joseph's plan "A" wasn't looking so good.

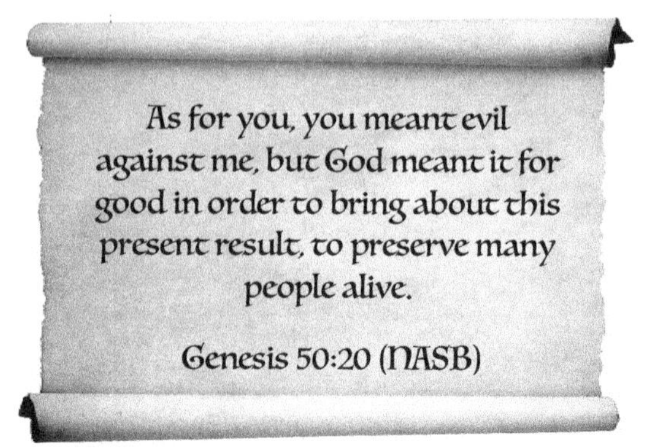

You likely know that God had a plan "B" for Joseph that turned out pretty awesome. He eventually does pull the golden ticket and gets handed the keys – not to a chocolate factory – to most of the Egyptian Empire. Even if you like chocolate, running an empire is way, way, way, better. What you may not know is that it took 13 years – Joseph's late teens and all of his 20's – for God's plan "A" to be fully revealed.

Why does it take so long for God to answer your prayers and bring along his best for you? It's you. You need some work before you are ready to step into God's plan "A" for your life. Joseph was undoubtedly praying while sitting in the hole his brothers dropped him in. How good of a ruler would Joseph have been if God plucked him out of that hole and dropped him in Egypt? Not so good. He'd still be a spoiled brat. But God's plan allowed for a way to prepare him for great things ahead.

Maybe you have spent your late teens and most of your 20's wondering what God's plan was for your life. Don't give up praying. Keep rolling. God's plan "A" may be just around the corner. Perhaps the caravan has come along to take you to the next step in God's plan, but you resisted. You're insisting on staying in the hole because you decided to stick with *your* plan "A". When a change of plans comes along, as hard as change may be, keep in mind that it might be *God's* plan "A". Then roll with it.

I'm sure it wasn't easy for Joseph to accept all the twists and turns in his life. But he continued to trust that God was working a plan and he kept rolling. Philip Yancy describes this kind of faith as, "Accepting in advance what will only make sense in reverse," in his book *Disappointment with God: Three Questions No One Asks Aloud* (Zondervan, 1988, 1992). When our plan "A" implodes it is easy to doubt, even curse God for not making our plan work. It is at those times that we need to be reminded that our plan "B" is very often God's plan "A" and we need to roll with it. Even though it feels pretty lousy when you're sitting at the bottom of a hole, looking back someday it will make sense.

TODAY'S CHALLENGE

1. **Eliminate Stinkin' Thinkin'**
   When life takes a turn for the worst does your mind immediately go to doubting God's faithfulness, saying He doesn't care? Honestly, that's the stinkin'-est type of thinking there is, because it turns our anger against the One who loves us the most. In those moments, we need to change our thinking to believing that God is working out a plan for us that we might only understand in reverse.

2. **Initiate Awesome Actions**
   The reason we get scared in times of trouble is because we doubt that God is looking out for us. To build your faith, study the passages from Scripture below on God's care for you:

   - God loves you like a father. Matthew 7:9-11, Psalm 103:13-14, Psalm 107:1
   - God works all things toward good for those that love Him. Romans 8:28, Ephesians 1:11
   - God gives strength, joy and peace. Psalm 29:11, Philippians 4:1-23, 1 Peter 5:6, Psalm 16, Psalm 23
   - God knows what you are going through. Psalm 34:15, Genesis 16:13. Psalm 34, Psalm 139:2-12
   - God Delivers me. Psalm 91, Psalm 34:7, John 16:33

   Then, just like building physical strength, you've got to exercise your faith to help it grow stronger. That means the next time plan "A" falls through and you have to move on to plan "B", accept in advance that God is working on your behalf – even thanking Him for this new opportunity – and just roll with it until you find out what good things God has in store you.

Clark Gerhart

"The best is yet to come."

Have you ever felt like you're on top of the world? Like you're flying high, can't be defeated, and nothing could ever bring you down? Well, you ain't seen nothing yet. The best is yet to come.

Have you ever felt like you're in the lowest of lows? Like you can't take one more punch, one more hit? Like your life is spiraling out of control and there's nothing that can ever change that? Take heart, because the best is yet to come.

Of all the quotes that I remember Scott repeating over and over, this was one of the ones I heard the most. It's not a Scott original. The great … a'hem … "theologian" Frank Sinatra, actually made it popular in his song, appropriately titled "The Best Is Yet to Come" from his 1964 album *It Might as Well Be Swing*. (and no, I'm not some avid Frank Sinatra fan... Google is just a thing). Scott used it so often, however, that he made it his own. It was basically his mantra.

When Frank Sinatra said it, it was wishful thinking based on budding romance. When Scott said it, it was hope-filled truth built on a promise interwoven all throughout Scripture. For those of us who follow Christ, we have a promise from the Almighty God, the author, creator, and sustainer of life, the one who breathes out galaxies and stars. In other words, a guy with the power to keep His promises! That promise is that He is actively working to prepare something for us that goes beyond our wildest expectations.

If God wasn't kidding, and the best really is yet to come, then you and I ought to be the most faith-filled, hopeful people on the planet. And, our hope is two-pronged.

The first facet of this hope is for my life here and now. Whether in my job, my church, my marriage, my friendships, or my life's calling, I can have hope that the best is yet to come if I am willing to have faith, walk with God in obedience, and continue the grind day-in and day-out. Even when "good" and "better" do not look the way we expect them to, His promise still stands: He will make all things work together for the good of those who love Him (Romans 8:28). That means everything. If it ain't good, God ain't done. The best is yet to come.

But even more than that, while we have *hope* that the best is yet to come in many areas of our lives, we have *assurance* that the best is yet to come when looking at the whole of our existence. You and I were not made to live temporary lives, but eternal ones. Every one of us will live forever … somewhere. Our time on earth is just a blink compared to our existence on the other side of eternity. And, if you are following Christ, Paul is quick to point out that God is preparing a place for you unlike anything you can imagine. In fact, as Scott would say, "You'd pee yourself if you got even a glimpse of it right now."

> No eye has seen, no ear has heard, and no mind has imagined what God has prepared for those who love him.
>
> 1 Corinthians 2:9b (NLT)

No matter what happens here, for better or worse, our stories are only beginning. Whether we experience the greatest days on earth or the worst days on earth, they're a blip on the radar of eternity. Our best days on earth can't even touch our worst days in Heaven … if there even is such a thing as a *worst day* in Heaven!.

In the ups and downs of life, wherever you are at, it is only for a season. It might be a terribly difficult season, or it might be an extremely joyous season. It might be a short season, or it might last your whole life. But it is only a season. Which is why it is always so refreshing to me whenever I am reminded of Scott's constant encouragement, "The best is yet to come."

That's not an exaggeration, it's not wishful thinking, for those of us walking with Jesus. With God at our side in this life, and an unimaginably wonderful place on the horizon in the next life, the best really is yet to come.

TODAY'S CHALLENGE

1. **Eliminate Stinkin' Thinkin'**
   Do you ever get so caught up in the past or the present that you stop being hopeful for the future? We usually lose hope for the future when we doubt that God has good things ahead for us. In those times, let's turn our thinking around and remember that God promises to work all things together for our good on earth (Romans 8:28) and has mind-blowingly awesome things for us on the other side of eternity (1 Corinthians 2:9).

2. **Initiate Awesome Actions**
   Find a place you will see every day and physically post a sign that says THE BEST IS YET TO COME where it can serve as a daily reminder that God is at work. Memorize 1 Corinthians 2:9 and Romans 8:28 so those truths are already in your mind before thoughts of hopelessness attempt to creep back in. Then, hold onto them when discouragement comes knocking.

Brad Travelpiece

"Religion is about the church and what you do for it. The Gospel is about Jesus and what He did for you."

Jews and Muslims have one god each that they worship. Christians also have one god, but he is also 3 at the same time. Buddhists have somewhere between zero and ten gods (and none of them are named Buddha, FYI). If there was a "Who Has The Most Gods Game" the Hindus would win with 330 million. Yup, I said 330 million. It's kind of like the Trinity ... but times 110 million.

Religions are very different. And, if you really get into their theology, religions become very, very, very different.

One of the things they all have in common, though, is rules.

Catholics can drink alcohol, and even do it in church. But it's 1920's prohibition time for Muslims. If you're a Rastafarian you gotta smoke pot. It's pretty much a rule. If you're a Baptist and you get caught with a bong in the back seat of your car – Oh, your friend left it there? Riiiight. Doesn't matter – you're getting hauled up front to confess your sin.

I'm not bashing any particular religion ... and, yes, I totally adulterated lots of theology ... I'm just saying religions have lots of rules. In fact, rules define just about all groups of people. Whether it's a church, a job, the Boy Scouts, or the Taylor Swift fan club, to get inside you have to follow the rules that the organization tells you to follow.

Scott wanted to make sure we remembered that following Christ is not about doing something to be part of a group ... it's about God sending His Son to save the people of the world, not condemn them because they didn't follow rules (John 3:16-17).

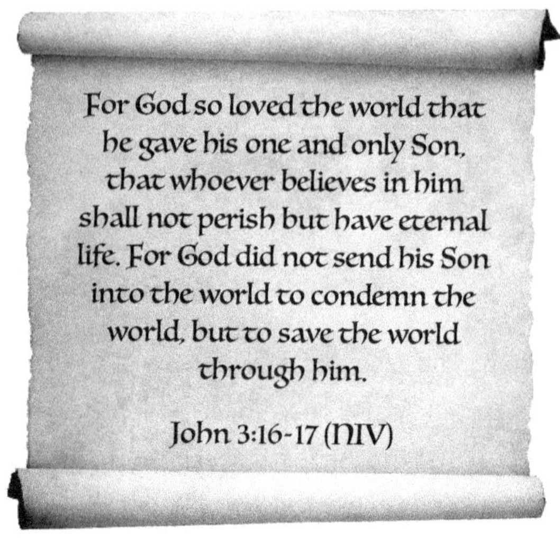

That's what makes Christianity different. Darren Whitehead and Jon Tyson, in their book *Rumors of God* (Thomas Nelson, 2012), tell us about a time when some religious professor types were sitting around discussing exactly this. I'm picturing a dimly lit room with leather chairs and bookcases filled with books lining the walls. "After much discussion, C. S. Lewis (a renowned Christian scholar) walked into the room and they asked him, 'What is the major difference between Christianity and other religions?' 'That's simple,' he replied. 'It's grace.' And then he left the room." If he had a mic I'm sure he dropped it as he left.

It's simple. Religion is about what you do to be a member of a church. But the Gospel of Christ is about what Jesus did to provide grace for us.

So, why does it feel like we still live by rules as Christians? Why do I feel like God might kick me out of the group whenever I break one?

There are probably lots of reasons for different people. It might surprise you, but one important cause is the Bible … or at least the misuse of the Bible. Andy Stanley tells us in his book *Irresistible* (Zondervan, 2018), "When it comes to what's in the Bible, the Old Testament is one of the primary stumbling blocks for non- and post-Christians. The Old Testament is used far more than the New Testament to create doubt in the minds of undergrad and graduate students."

The Old Testament … *a stumbling block to people getting the message of grace*. Hmmm. You don't hear that every day.

Stanley says that too often we give young people – like me as a graduating high school senior – a leather bound, gold edged, name embossed Bible. Then we tell them that it's the infallible word of God from contents to maps. That means that the covenant of rules in the Old Testament carries the same weight as the covenant of grace in the New Testament. Thus, rules are still important for being in the club.

What they didn't tell us, or didn't make clear, is that the old agreement was infallible in its day, but it became obsolete (Hebrews 8:13). All the rules – hundreds and hundreds of them – that made up the contract between God and man no longer apply. Christ made a new agreement with mankind based on what He did, not what we do (Hebrews 9:15). And it's simple. It's Grace. And that's irresistible.

This is not a trivial theological point. This can mean the difference between a person experiencing God's love or living with mixed messages that they still have to perform to receive God's love and redemption. That's why it is so important to be reminded that the Gospel is not about what we do to be part of religion. The Gospel is about Jesus and what He did for us.

That doesn't mean the Old Testament is worthless. It still has value for helping us understand God and the history of our faith. We have relied on it throughout this book, just as Scott did throughout his teachings. But we have to be clear: Rules are no longer the way to relationship with God. Grace is.

What about all the instructions in the New Testament, then? Aren't they just a new set of rules? Fortunately, someone asked Jesus exactly that when he was on earth and He made it crystal clear that all the rules melted down to just two. The most important one is loving God. The second is loving people. Everything you do when following Christ depends on these two things … which together depend on one: Love (Matthew 22:36-40). Any instructions for living outlined in the New Testament depend on this love. Repeatedly lists of instructions are clarified that we do them, "just as Christ also loved us" (Ephesians 5:2,

5:25), or because we *are* followers of Christ's Gospel of love not *to become* followers of Christ (Galatians 2:20).

We don't abstain from murdering people, committing adultery, stealing, lying, or coveting because they are rules written on stone tablets that we must do to be part of a religion. We don't do those things because that wouldn't be love. God loved us and sent Jesus to save us. Now, we live expressing that love to others.

TODAY'S CHALLENGE

1. **Eliminate Stinkin' Thinkin'**
   Examine your feelings for a moment. Do you feel guilt or fear over violating a Christian rule? Do you look down on others whose lives are full of sinful behavior? Do you believe Christians are distinguished from other people in the world by their behavior? Think about the last one carefully. We all expect a Christian's behavior to be noticeably improved … but is that what tells other people we follow Christ? No. Love is (John 13:35). These can be deep, subtle, ingrained traces of Old Covenant thinking seeping into your New Covenant relationship with God through Christ.

2. **Initiate Awesome Actions**
   Take out your Bible. Open to the book of Matthew. Now tear the book in two. It is a powerful reminder that the Old and New Covenants are different as you read them. If that's too dramatic, just read them and remember the two are different. Live a life that pours out love, not because of religious rules, because Christ loved you first.

Clark Gerhart

"You'll never move forward if you stay here...it's too comfortable."

I can count on one hand the pivotal moments in my life when someone I trust had a direct conversation that rattled my perspective and immediately changed the course of my journey. One of them was the fall of 2011 … Scott and his wife Brenda were over, enjoying a dinner with our family out on our deck. Like all of our meals together, the appetizer was sprinkled with sarcastic jokes and frequent laughter, but the main course conversation is what really filled me up.

I had just finished recording my first solo album and was wrestling through the decision of whether to take an opportunity to move to Nashville. I was battling fears of financial survival, along with a complete restructuring of life … new relationships, new job, new state … new everything. Scott patiently listened to all my concerns, offering some empathetic courtesy-statements like, "I get that, "Yeah, it's hard," and some," "Uh huh, sure." But then he lined me up in his crosshairs. I'm not sure if he was aiming for my head or my heart, but he knew which I needed at the time. He had reached the point, like he so often did, where he couldn't handle the counselor ploy anymore … you know, when they just listen and allow you to come to your own conclusion. No, I was getting caught in the vortex of recycling fears and there was no way I was climbing out on my own. He knew it was time to hit me right between the eyes with truth.

He casually leaned back in his chair with his hands folded behind his head, and said, "Dude, you have to go. Get out of this house. You'll never move forward if you stay here … it's too comfortable."

In that moment, I was shocked, to be honest. I wasn't shocked in an offended way … it was refreshing. I wasn't expecting someone to just tell me what to do. People aren't usually that direct when it comes to advice on a huge life decision. But it came from someone who knew me enough to have wisdom on the situation, and we had built enough trust that he could give it to me straight. Honestly, those bold words were the confirmation of what I had already felt in my spirit. God was telling me to go, but I was waylaid by doubt, fear, and comfort. In an instant the clouds blew away and I felt clarity.

Dang.

I was dumbfounded. My eyes widened. I sat up ready to reply but had nothing to say. There was nothing more to discuss. I finally had the green light to follow God's call. It sounds funny that you would need a signal … like a traffic signal … to decide to follow God, but that's exactly how I felt. Like I was stuck at an intersection and finally the red light blinked off and I got the signal to move on.

It's ironic how, when faced with the fear of the unknown, we resort to processing all the details in an attempt to eliminate all of our fears *before* we step into where God is calling us. Being courageous does not remotely mean having it all figured out. This is the time to be strong and courageous…just like Joshua. Which means choosing to trust that when God said, "I'll be with you wherever you go," He actually meant it. It means being bold and taking action even when it takes you out of your comfort zone. And, it's not just a cute suggestion or inspirational quote that's meant to merely stay on some adorable wall hanging you bought from TJ Maxx.

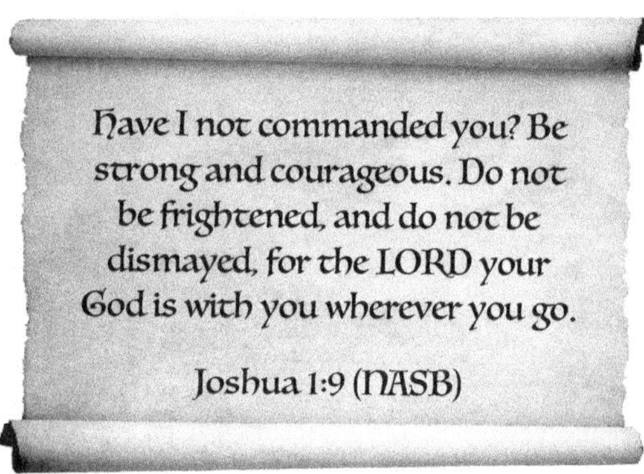

(Yeah, I have those, too.) He's not *suggesting* you consider being strong and courageous if you feel like it. He *commands* it.

God desperately wants us to step out of the boat like Peter did … or step out of Pennsylvania like I did. … and He doesn't take that lightly. Eternities are at stake. We cannot permit our silly irrational fears on earth to steal from the greater purposes to which God has called us.

Maybe you have a spirit nudge towards a huge decision that you're putting off because you're afraid … or because you're comfortable right where you're at. God promises to be with you wherever you go. And, as the common saying goes, "If He led you into it, He'll lead you through it." So be strong and courageous!

Maybe you don't have someone like Scott who knows you well and you trust, who can call you out on a big decision you're avoiding. If you don't, you should try to find a person who does. Until you do, let me be the one to lovingly tell you:

YOU HAVE TO GO. YOU'LL NEVER MOVE FORWARD IF YOU STAY HERE!

TODAY'S CHALLENGE

1. **Eliminate Stinkin' Thinkin'**
   Where is fear holding you back? It sure would stink if you missed living your best life, possible because you were afraid to step out into something uncomfortable, even scary, to find God's best. When your mind naturally starts to fear, remember that God promises to be with you wherever you go … and then get going!

2. **Initiate Awesome Actions**
   You will likely reach many intersections in life where you feel stuck and need someone to get you going, like Scott did for me. Find that Scott-like person in your life who knows you and cares about you enough to speak into your life. If you don't have one, look for one. A pastor or other mentor from church can be a great option. Maybe a friend or sibling. How about your aunt or uncle? You know, the cool ones. Every family has them. They know a lot about you but don't have the direct family-of-origin baggage. Or, strange as it may be to suggest, your parents … or even grandparents … that you've been dismissing because you think they're too old to understand what you're going through? Human life hasn't changed as much as you think in the last few decades. They probably have experienced similar things to what you are going through. Plus, they have known you since they were changing your diapers! Make a habit of discussing important decisions with your Scott-like person and look for the green lights that God gives you through them.

Brooke Gerhart

"Bad is temporary. Good is eternal."

Somewhere among the courses I took in college for my biology degree was a course called Human Growth and Development. As instructive as it was, it was nothing like watching it happen as our four children grew from childhood to adulthood, then to having kids of their own. And now that I have reached the pinnacle of human development and have started down the other side, I guess I have experienced most of what humans go through as they grow and develop.

One thing I have learned is that every stage of human development has one similar component: troubles.

It starts when you're one year old and your big sister is getting candy and the people handing out the treats refuse to give you any. I remember my own kids suffering through this immense, earth shattering injustice. The looks of emotional anguish on their little faces expressed the most intense sadness and sense of unfairness. They had no idea what those hard little balls of sugar or rubbery wads of gum would do when they became lodged in their tiny windpipes. They couldn't comprehend that Dad was actually blessing them by *not* giving them candy. Nevertheless, they cry and wail from the their gut-wrenching, soul-rending pain. Such anguish at this early stage of development!

The troubles only get bigger from there. Later, the struggles come as failed math tests, lost boyfriends, and missed soccer goals. I chuckle to myself as I hear young parents complaining about dealing with the problems of young children. Just wait, I think to myself, in a few years it could be failed drug tests, lost spouses, and missed menstrual periods. Ah, yes. Human growth and development gets harder as you go.

The worst thing about the troubles we experience in life is that while they are happening, they consume us. All of our attention and emotional energy gets sucked into the vortex that surrounds the problem. We become that screaming toddler who can't see past the fact that he isn't getting what he wants. Who never considers that there might be a bigger reason for why the nice lady who holds him every day … and changes his diaper many times a day … and has been feeding him as long as he can remember … is suddenly withholding something from him. He can see only his lack of candy and that mommy is failing him. Unfortunately, that's pretty much you and me in the midst of many (most? all?) of our bad times.

Just at that moment, when all we can see is bad, it is time to remember that bad is temporary, but good is eternal.

I like how Paul refers to our troubles as "light and momentary." He makes no distinction. He means all of them. In fact, he said this in the middle of the persecution of the early church. Christians were being beaten, imprisoned, and killed. Families were torn apart. Financial ruin. You name it. So, there is no saying, "Well, he didn't know what I would go through. He didn't know how bad I would have it." He knew. And still, Paul calls all these troubles "light and momentary" because bad is temporary, good is eternal.

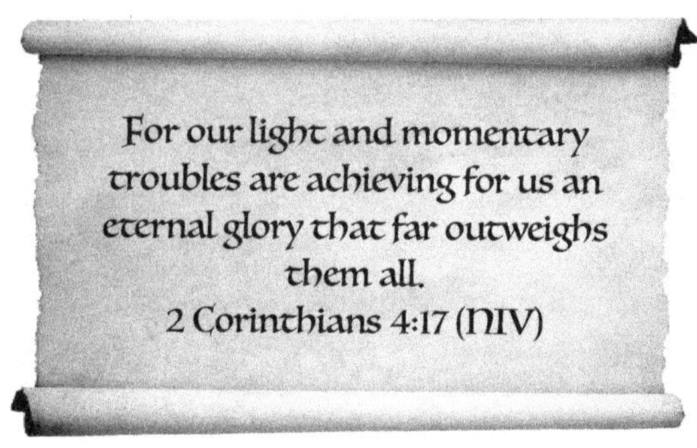

What is the worst, nightmarish trouble you could experience? It will end. It might not end quickly. It might not end well. To be sure, this world is a big smelly pile of chocolate ice cream emoji (wink) as a result of the corruption of sin. It is not a nice place much of the time. But our world is temporal, that is, governed by time. And time is a relentless river continually pushing you forward. You have a big test … job interview … difficult conversation with a friend … the next day, next week, next month? Time will push you through it. Bad is temporary. God, however, is not temporal. He's eternal … and He's good. If you are following the math, that adds up to: bad is temporary and good is eternal.

Some problems don't have an end date, like dealing with severe illness or watching a loved one struggle to find purpose or waiting to find a spouse. If they never ended for your entire life and you got to go to heaven after it all, would that be okay? Certainly, life is not a sitcom. Not every problem we face will be perfectly resolved by the end of the show. Even with that unpleasant reality, we can live faithfully, even joyfully, in the midst of problems because we know that God's love for us is eternal. It is there caring for us when we can't see it. It is there in all of the nurture and provision you and I take for granted on all the good days. It is protecting us from the shiny, tasty stuff we cry out to get that would ultimately suffocate and destroy us if we got them. It is there all of your life …and my life… and for all of eternity because God is good and God is eternal.

TODAY'S CHALLENGE

1. **Eliminate Stinkin' Thinkin'**
   Consider the bad things you are worried about right now. Do any of them feel like they will never end? Do you feel like a current problem is finally the one that is going to wipe you out completely? That thinking doesn't sound like someone who has God at their side with all the time in the world to work things out. It may be a very tough time … maybe very, very tough. Keep the positive mind-set that God will be there with you through it all … eternally.

2. **Initiate Awesome Actions**
   If the thing that is weighing on you right now has an end date, do the best you can with the time you have to deal with it, but recognize that the things you fear in your future will soon be memories of your past. Instead of letting fear paralyze you, work on a contingency plan if things don't go well. If you are failing all your tests in this class, you might need to change your major. When that meeting with the boss goes poorly, it's probably time to rethink your career options. If that difficult conversation with a friend didn't result in a blinding flash of revelation and repentance … well, you're probably getting the idea by now ... it is time for some friendship boundaries.

   And, when it looks like problems will go unsolved, recognize that sometimes God has something good in the works that we just can't see. Trust that He is good and will bring about good for you, either now or in eternity.

Clark Gerhart

"If we know that difficulties produce depth of character and endurance, why do we remove them from kids, rather than coach them through?"

God gave me an enormous gift when he trusted my wife, Pam, and me to rear two amazing daughters. Krysta and Alycia are my pride and joy. And, as most dads of girls can attest, I will literally do about anything to protect our beauties from pain and sorrow.

Krysta is the first-born, so all of Krysta's experiences were firsts in parenting for us. So, we made mistakes. The story I'm about to relate was one of those times that I didn't get it quite right and needed help, even though I'd been parenting for two decades at that point.

That's where Scott came in. Here's the story:

If you had asked Krysta when she was little what she wanted to be in life, she would have told you without hesitation that she wanted to be a teacher. She stayed laser focused on that goal, graduated high school with honors and then sailed through college earning dual degrees in both Education and English. She was ready to be that teacher she always dreamed of being. Then, she just had to convince a school administrator that she was ready.

She interviewed at an area high school in a school district she very much wanted to work in. Following the interview, she had high hopes. Then came the bad news. She didn't get the job. I knew she'd be sad … and she was. Heck, I was sad. All I ever needed to see were tears welling-up in my girls' eyes and I became a pool of melted butter.

I immediately flew into "fixer" mode. So, I referred her to Scott. Who better, I thought, to help me make Krysta feel better than her pastor with whom she already had a good relationship? I was sure he could give her the *back in the saddle* talk and get her back on the track of success.

I picked up the phone and called him that day to fill him in about Krysta. I asked him if he wouldn't mind saying a few words of encouragement to her. How he replied, made me think hard for a minute. He said, "You know, it probably won't hurt her to take a few swings and a miss every now and then."

Hmmm. Not what I expected.

Scott volunteered as a coach, so the sports reference didn't surprise me. He invested much into the young people he interacted with in our area. He was used to preparing kids for the game of life. He reminded me that day that the best thing that I could do for Krysta in the moment was to help her push through the disappointment and learn how to frame the loss in the context of the bigger picture of where her Godly purpose lies. There was something better awaiting.

Why didn't I think of that? My first reaction was to remove the difficulty from her life and try to shield her from the pain. Not smart!

Paul reminded the Corinthians of the same thing. He used a sports reference, too, and knew it would resonate with his Greek, Olympic-minded friends. He encouraged them to remain disciplined and reach for an eternal prize by running, "… with purpose in every step." Notice that he tells them … and us … that there is purpose in *every* step, even the tough ones. So, steering our kids away from the difficult parts of the process would allow them

All athletes are disciplined in their training. They do it to win a prize that will fade away, but we do it for an eternal prize. So, I run with purpose in every step.

1 Corinthians 9:25-26 (NLT)

to miss important steps along the way. It would be like telling an athlete that they could skip their workouts if they are too difficult. No, good coach … or good parent … would do that!

While eulogizing his father, former President George W. Bush said of George H.W. Bush, "He encouraged and comforted but never steered." Your role is to teach and support, not steer. Whatever they encounter along the way will help them grow stronger … like that athlete in training … if you coach them through the experience. Plus, you may be butting into God's better plan for their lives.

It's important that we parents teach our children the value of discipline in life while pointing our children to find the purpose that God created them to fulfill. And, in case you were wondering, God had a much better plan for Krysta in the end. The principal who interviewed her recommended her for a position in a neighboring district where she is thriving. Her students love her and she loves them. She made it to her goal of becoming a teacher … although, not in the school district she expected … and has a greater depth of character and more endurance by persevering through the race to get to the prize.

TODAY'S CHALLENGE

1. **Eliminate Stinkin' Thinkin'**
   When your kids struggle, does your brain immediately go to fixing the problem, like me? Maybe you're a helicopter parent, hovering over your kids, finding ways to make life easier. That approach seems very nice and supportive, but it is actually stinkin' thinkin'. You have to come to grips with the fact that saving your kids from every discomfort … even the pain of failure … is actually weakening them. It will make them less able to deal with difficulties in the future, when you are not there to drop in and rescue them.

2. **Initiate Awesome Actions**
   Teach your kids the *swing and miss* concept. Not every hit is a homerun. Even the best ballplayers strike out once in a while. Help them see that it is okay to fail once in a while, and that those defeats can help them grow stronger in the process. To reinforce the concept, share your story. Do your children know about the times you pushed through difficulties? Be as open as you can be with them. Be intentional about making time to be with them to have those conversations. You'll be surprised what they will learn from your stories … even your failures … as they gain a new understanding of how you arrived at today's life destination.

Chuck Humphrey

"Because other people's eternity is more important than our today."

Why do you play guitar music in our church when I'm so moved by hymns? Why don't you wear a suit and tie to show respect to God? How could you possibly play a secular song as an intro in your sanctuary? Why in the world would you talk about money and sex and relationships in a sermon? Why can't you just teach the Bible verse by verse? Scott was asked these questions many times … over and over … and would answer, "Because other people's eternity is more important than our today."

Let's face it, many people don't like church. Some have had bad experiences in the past. Some were tired of being smacked in the back of the head when they made noise. And, I suspect, tons of people feel in church like I felt when I decided to experience a NASCAR race for the first time. All the race fans around me were super excited about which driver was racing and what team had the most points. They knew whose car was running tight … who had the high groove … why they decided on a short pit … how a driver had just performed a slingshot. To me it was just cars driving in circles. I never went to another race.

We don't want exploring a life following Christ to feel like me trying NASCAR. I definitely did not become a believer. So, we try to make as many people as possible feel comfortable at church. At times, that means giving up some of the stuff that makes *us* feel comfortable at church. After all, giving up feeling good today to help others feel good for eternity is always more than a fair trade.

How about working together with other Christian churches in your area to reach people for Christ? The answer too often is, "They have different doctrine than us! How could you even suggest that?!"

Because other people's eternity is more important than our today.

Why don't you try working with non-religious charities in your area because they can run a soup kitchen better than you can? You can still be there as a Christian and demonstrate Christ's love for the needy. "Never!" some would say. "Working with anyone but Christians is wrong."

Not if other people's eternity is more important than our today.

Many of us in our churches are not so happy about giving up our today. We like our church just the way it is right now. After all, isn't that why we go? We like the messages and the music. We see our Christian friends. We are fed the scriptures there. We even have our favorite seat picked out. Why disrupt all that?

Because if it is keeping other people from experiencing God's love, then it is impacting their eternity, and ... you guessed it ... other people's eternity is more important than our today.

Would you avoid religious jargon when talking to people who didn't know churchy lingo? Can you make the message of Christ as appealing at the country club gala as it would be at dart night at Bunker's Sports Bar and Grille (great hot wings BTW). Would you be willing to be vulnerable with your failings to help encourage someone else who is struggling in a similar way? The answer should be, "Yes!" because… you get it … I'm not even going to say it.

> I have become all things to all people so that by all possible means I might save some.
>
> 1 Corinthians 9: 22 (NIV)

Some of this is hard to hear and may even sound unbiblical because we have been taught that the Bible tells us to act churchy. Paul said the opposite. And he wrote a lot of the Bible. He said he was willing to give up his way of doing things and adopt other people's ways so that everyone could hear the message of Christ so that some might be saved.

My wife and I experienced an example of how this can go wrong in our churches. We had just moved to town and were looking for a new church. We were corralling four young kids into the foyer of a new prospect. We looked as lost as a 13-year-old boy who followed his Mom into the women's underwear section of JC Penny. We didn't know where to look and searched for a friendly face to direct us to children's classrooms. One woman stopped her conversation with a group of her Christian friends to glance over at us. I opened my expression pleadingly. She looked us up and down and turned back to her conversation. My wife and I eyed each other with cringe-face emoji looks and turned and left.

What if we were non-Christians standing in the entrance way to a new life of faith in Christ? What if we looked pleadingly for help, not knowing where to start, and found nothing but comfy Christians focused on each other? What if we had turned and left behind a chance at having our eternities affected, and those of our kids, because Christians were not willing to give up their todays?

TODAY'S CHALLENGE

1. **Eliminate Stinkin' Thinkin'**
   Do you look forward to Sunday mornings as a time to connect with your Christian friends? I'd like you to consider that our churches are really a place to gather in the surrounding community, not just the community of believers. It is not a coincidence that churches traditionally have been placed in the middle of towns. That's so they are readily available to people who want to find a place to get to know God. We even put steeples on them so you can see from across town where to go when you are ready for a spiritual encounter.

Do you view your church as a place where you go to get "fed" spiritually? If so, it's time to adjust that. Take off your bib and climb down out of your high chair. You're a grownup. You can feed yourself. Sunday morning services have only enough time to introduce people to Christ who have never met Him and inspire Christ followers to know Him better. Personal study, prayer and joining with other Christians throughout the week is where real spiritual growth and learning happens. Rethink Sunday mornings and how you can make them about other people's eternity, not just your today.

2. **Initiate Awesome Actions**

Look around your church this weekend and try to view it through the eyes of someone who has never been to church. Look at the physical space and what people are doing. Listen to the music and the message. If you hadn't been used to being there, would it attract or repel you from the Gospel? If it would repel you, let someone know. You'll take some heat for it when you do. It's ok. It's not about *you* anyway.

Here's another exercise: Stay away from your friends this Sunday. Look for strangers and talk to them. Some of your friends won't like it. It's ok. It's not about *them* anyway. Now let's put this on steroids … next Sunday, invite the friends you avoided last Sunday to join you in talking with new people who are visiting that Sunday. Once again, you'll probably catch some heat. But… that's right… so what … it's about other people's eternity!

Clark Gerhart

"Trust isn't earned. It's a gift."

"Seth, someone told me today that they heard you've been getting drunk with your friends. I don't believe it, but I wanted to hear it from you". Dad laid that on me through a clenched jaw when he came home from work one day. My heart dropped. I could feel the apprehension in his voice resonating in my chest. But the truth was, I had been drinking. When I fessed up, he had to turn and walk away. He started to break down before he made it out of the room. I sat there stunned as remorse and shame fought in my heart to see which would draw tears first.

I had enjoyed close to complete freedom living in my parents' house to that point, but I lost some privileges after that. I wasn't allowed to go certain places. I wasn't allowed to stay out through the night. And I didn't deserve those liberties. I had abused my parents' trust.

A few weeks later my parents sat me down in our living room. I could see that they were still hurt. Despite that, they restored to me the freedoms they had taken. I was blown away and couldn't understand why. Dad told me that he was learning that trust isn't earned, it's a gift.

My parents knew that I would be on my own soon and setting my own boundaries. They decided to entrust that freedom to me early so that I would have time to gain confidence and wisdom before I was off on my own. They knew I had made mistakes, and probably would make more (I did) but they saw the bigger picture. They empowered the man I could become instead of crippling the boy that I was.

The decision my parents made had a huge impact on me for two reasons. The first hit me right away. They believed in me. They would have kept certain freedoms from me if they didn't think I would learn to manage them. But they knew I could. Because of that, I believed I could too. The second was the grace to be patient with me while I learned to handle the responsibility that I wasn't quite ready for. They recognized that to grow, you have to be in over your head sometimes.

God has been giving the same gift of trust since the very beginning. He spent six days building a more beautiful world than you can imagine, and shortly after, He handed the keys to the Kingdom over to Adam. Adam had no experience or qualifications to run the Garden of Eden. He didn't have a polished resume, or a spiffy LinkedIn profile. What he did have was a father who empowered him to be all that he could be. Who walked with him while he figured it out. Adam didn't do anything to deserve his rulership, God just gave it to him. And yes, Adam messed up. God knew he would. But He was more interested in developing His ongoing relationship with Adam ... along with all of mankind that he spawned. He would create a way to redeem mankind and preserve His perfect creation, later, through Christ.

I still did some stupid things after my parents restored my freedom. But I knew that the trust they gave me was a gift. A gift I wanted to use well. It took time, but I learned to set good boundaries, and eventually to use my freedom to build others up and not just seek my own pleasure. I'm a better man because of it. That was the power of the gift my parents gave me.

You've been given a similar gift by your Heavenly Father. He has entrusted to you the message of His love and pursuit of people, the keys to his new Kingdom on earth. There is no greater responsibility! You might feel in over your head sometimes and you'll make some mistakes, but God gave it to you as a gift to help you grow. He's given you everything you need to deliver his message. And he believes in you!

Luke 12:32 tells us that it's God's pleasure to give you the Kingdom. That means not only does He offer you this gift, He delights to see you take ownership of it. Because, then He gets to enjoy watching you follow after Him in new ways as you pour yourself out into your family, your co-workers, and your friends. To see you make yourself vulnerable, in order to build deeper relationships within your circles of influence and share the hope you have in Christ. He's even glad to see you try when you know you might screw it up and loves to see you try again when you do mess up. He is with you for every step, clearing the way, equipping you for the task, and encouraging you to press on. Make yourself available to Him in obedience and He will build His Kingdom on earth as He reigns in you.

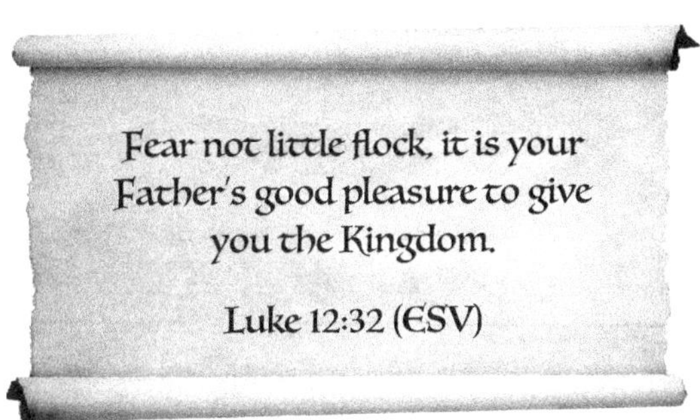

God chose to entrust to you the mission nearest to His heart: Drawing those He loves into His Kingdom. Your efforts to build God's kingdom are the most effective means by which God builds His Kingdom into you. What an incredible plan and unbelievable gift. It could have only come from the heart of a loving father.

TODAY'S CHALLENGE

1. **Eliminate Stinkin' Thinkin'**
   Do you often feel shame and separation from God because of your screw ups? It is possibly due to a wrong impression of God. You need to see God as a loving father who wants to give us His trust and watch us succeed in it. When I failed my father's trust in high school, he gifted it back to me in order to restore full relationship. We have a Heavenly Father who does the same. Yes, He feels the disappointment any loving father feels when their child abuses that trust. But it doesn't end there. His fatherly love bursts out with joy when His child returns. He heaps love and blessing on them, erasing the mistrust and gifting them again with full relationship.

2. **Initiate Awesome Actions**
   Gifting trust to someone empowers them to be better people. It elevates them to a higher level of trustworthiness and motivates them to step into the role or task with which they have been trusted. God does that for us. Has God entrusted you with some new part to play in building His kingdom? Tell someone who will help you stay accountable to that trust. Then do it!

   Also, recognize that you can empower others by gifting trust to them. It could be anyone who looks up to you or you are responsible for: a child, an employee, a younger believer. Entrust something important to them and empower them to handle it. If they fail, remember, it's about their development, not the success of the thing. Walk through the process with them in good relationship.

Seth Fetterolf

"I'd rather struggle for contentment than live an 'ignorance is bliss' life."

Scott and I were both processing significant changes in our careers. Scott had given up control of the church where he was senior pastor to become part of a large multi-campus church. I was giving up my private surgical practice to become part of a large multi-specialty physician group. We both were letting go of what was comfortable in order to accomplish bigger, and hopefully better, things. The concerns over loss of autonomy and fear of abandoning a mission were remarkably similar. As we wrestled with these various feelings together, I texted Scott to say, "No matter what choice I make, my own heart and brain will be there to deal with, and I'll have to fight the battle for contentment, no doubt. That has been a lifelong battle. I don't think I have the chemistry for contentment, but I'm trying!"

"Me too!" Scott responded, "I still think I'd rather struggle with contentment than live and 'ignorance is bliss' life."

You see what Scott did there, right? He just drew a horizontal line with the over achievers on one side and blissful ignorance on the other. We all exist on this line somewhere. Scott and I admitted on that day that we were decidedly on the achieve-aholics side. I can think of a handful of people I know who are just as surely on the hang-loose-and-let-someone-else-worry-about-it end of life.

So, which end of the spectrum is right?

I can tell you first hand that the achiever end of the scale is filled with very productive people who are typically stressed out and who rarely stop to smell the roses. They … actually I should say *we* because this is my crowd … tend to live in houses and drive cars that are too expensive for us. When you ask us for help, we always have to consult our Google calendar first. But we will help because it gives us a goal. Unfortunately, chasing that new goal distracts us from accomplishing our fourteen other projects and that makes us even more stressed out.

The blissful end of the scale … at least, I've been told. I've never actually visited this end … is populated with people who don't even know that ROI is "a thing" because they don't really care that every expenditure has a return on investment. They typically can be found chilling out and they rarely smell like roses because bathing puts toxic detergents into the environment. Their car is also too expensive for them – but they live in it. When you ask them for help, they will also always say, "Yes" but often don't show up. Especially if it interferes with their chill time.

Did you see yourself in any of those descriptions? Don't worry, it's only tongue-in-cheek descriptions. Plus, it doesn't matter anyway. Neither is right. This is the continuum under *the bell curve of life*. And just like the bell curve that might have been used to determine your test grade in school, there are people spread throughout the range. The middle of the curve is where everyone gets a "C." Which in this case stands for *contentment*.

Contentment. The middle ground of balance for which we all strive. Paul was able to find the center "C". He said in Philippians 4:12, "I know what it is to be in need, and I know what it is to have plenty." Apparently, he's been at both ends of this socio-economic bell curve of life. And remarkably, he found the middle, saying, "I have learned the secret of being *content* in any and every situation."

Very few of us live in perfect contentment, so we tend to fall off the curve to one side or the other. I already told you that I tend toward the always-striving-for-more end. Either side you tend to roll off onto has both pros and cons. People who are perfectly satisfied to pitch a tent somewhere and stay put would probably never design a rocket to go to the moon. But the rocket scientists who have only ever written a computer algorithm will likely never write a sonnet. Whether you strive for upper levels of management or upper levels of Minecraft, own it, just like Scott owned his tendency toward discontentment. It's part of being you.

Here is something Paul tells us we should never be content with, however: our pursuit of a life with God. In Philippians 3:12 he tells us that he wasn't content with his progress toward his goal of being Christ-like. This is the same guy from a few paragraphs up this page who said he was "content in any and every situation." He found contentment on the socio-economic scale … then he left that scale behind. He gave up worrying about whether he was rich or poor and began striving to grab hold of more of Christ. He goes on to say that he would never be content that he had arrived at his spiritual goal. He would press on until he reached heaven and was made perfect.

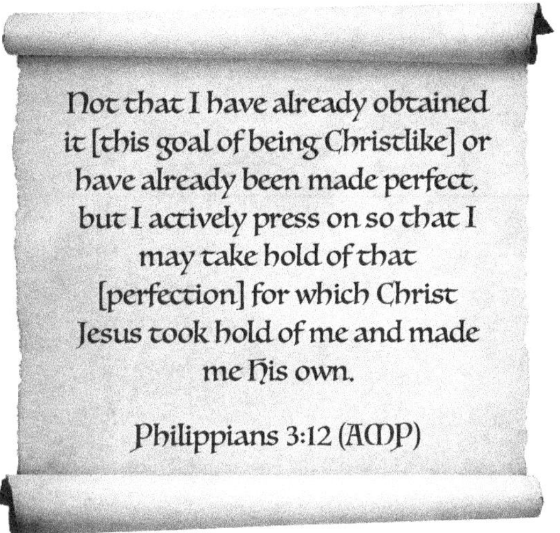

Scott likewise would not be content with his spiritual progress until he reached perfection. Far better to live with some discontentment, than to live in ignorant bliss, hoping that our spiritual condition will all workout fine in the end somehow, without any attention here and now.

To accomplish spiritual maturity, we can't be content with where we are at, we have to actively pursue it. We spend a lot of energy trying to improve our standing on society's socio-economic curve. We need to commit as much effort advancing on the spiritual progress curve. You might be a genius professionally but a flunky spiritually. You might be working hard to become more Zen in your personal life but not really becoming more Christ-like in your spiritual life. If either is true of you, redirect some energy to making spiritual progress. And don't be content until you reach perfection in heaven!

TODAY'S CHALLENGE

1. **Eliminate Stinkin' Thinkin'**
   Where do you live on the contentment spectrum? It is okay to be who you are. And, you can appreciate, rather than disparage, people who might live at a different place on the contentment curve. But the world's contentment curve is really about the level of socio-economic success you are content to attain. Disconnect from that thinking for a bit and consider where you are on the spiritual progress curve. Adopt a lack-of-contentment attitude with your spiritual life. Let it motivate you to press on to more spiritual maturity.

2. **Initiate Awesome Actions**
   You likely spend a lot of resources pursuing earthly things to find contentment. Commit to spending energy pursuing God. Just like you would plan to succeed in other parts of life, plan to succeed spiritually. Schedule time in your phone or computer to read, pray, reflect, and be silent and listen to God to build relationship with Him. Schedule a meeting with others to discuss a spiritual action plan. Find a ministry project and invest some time, money and energy to produce spiritual ROI.

Clark Gerhart

"Happiness leaks."

In a sermon series called *Habits of Happiness* (based on a series by Rick Warren with the same name) Scott caught my attention with the short but dramatic statement, "Happiness leaks." During my entire life as a Christian I was told – either directly or implied – that the Joy of the Lord comes as a package deal with accepting Christ. And yet there were many times … actually many, many, many times … when I have not been filled with the unspeakable joy that the Lord is supposed to dispense. With this one striking statement, however, it all became clear.

We accept salvation and experience relief from guilt.

Then happiness leaks.

We enjoy the love and support of being in a new family of Christians.

Then happiness leaks.

We share our faith with others and bring joy to them and ourselves.

Then happiness leaks.

The joy of the Lord *is* part of a two-for-one special. Then life happens. The pressures of daily living squeeze the pleasant feelings out of us. We get confused. We wonder why we are missing the joy that was supposed to be a supernatural additive to our lives. Salvation was supposed to be like buying an Iced Skinny Cinnamon Dolce Latte from Starbucks. You get all that rich and creamy goodness without guilt because it's made with skim milk. Then, as if that wasn't enough, hidden inside is a mega dose of caffeine to really make your day sparkle. In other words, accept Christ and get rich and creamy goodness ... no guilt ... and sparkling with happiness.

Then happiness leaks.

The reason that happiness leaks is because joy doesn't come as a flavor-syrup that gets pumped into our spiritual latte. If you are praying for God to drizzle some supernatural happiness over your life – as I have done many times over the years – you can stop. It ain't happening. That's not the way joy works.

Joy is a "fruit of the spirit" that grows in our lives as we "walk in the Spirit." (Galatians 5:22-25) Like real fruit, spiritual fruit needs a good plant on which to grow. If apples aren't growing, the problem is in the health of the tree. If the fruit of joy isn't growing, the problem is in the health of our spiritual walk with God. Billy Sunday, one of America's most influential evangelists, said it this way, "If you lack joy, your Christianity must be leaking somewhere." We have found the source of the leak! When happiness is draining, we have to look at our walk with Christ and patch the holes in our Christianity to keep joy from trickling away.

> Always be full of joy in the Lord: I say it again, rejoice! Let everyone see that you are unselfish and considerate in all you do. Remember that the Lord is coming soon. Don't worry about anything: instead, pray about everything: tell God your needs, and don't forget to thank him for his answers.
>
> Philippians 4:4-6 (TLB)

Holes appear in our Christianity when we hold wrong beliefs. Or they appear when we hold accurate beliefs, but we don't let that truth *take hold of us*. We have already addressed the wrong belief that happiness automatically appears in a Christian's life. If we hold on to that mistruth we will miss the happiness that comes from walking in a spiritual relationship with Christ. OK, we got that.

Now we have to let that truth take hold of us. Paul gives us some very practical ways that we can "walk in the Spirit." He outlines them in his letter to the Christians living in Philippi. They thought these ideas were so helpful that they passed them on to other Christians, who passed them on to others, who passed them on to us, so that we could experience true joy, too. Let's unpack what Paul says in Philippians 4:4-6:

1. Be unselfish and considerate of others.
Depression and self-centeredness go hand-in-hand. When we're depressed all our thoughts get pulled inward and we become centered on us. We focus on the bad feelings we are experiencing, how uncomfortable they are and how we can escape them. It works in reverse, too. Self-centered living tends to *make* us depressed by driving people away – along with the joy that comes with relationship. When happiness is leaking, focus on other people and *their* needs. It will take your mind off of *your* needs and you will regain joy.

2. Keep an eternal perspective.
In the midst of struggles, Paul reminds us that the happiness-draining events that we are experiencing now will eventually end. And they will end in magnificent happiness when Christ takes us to heaven with Him. If we stay focused on that eternal perspective the difficulties of today don't seem so significant by comparison. As a result, they are less joy-stealing.

3. Pray about your problems instead of worrying.
Worry punches holes in our happiness bucket. When we worry, we see a situation in a negative light and predict that bad things will happen in the future. But we don't have to expect bad things. In fact, God promises that He can make good things happen out of any situation (Romans 8:28). If worry is draining your happiness, keep your mind busy praying about your problems to break the worry cycle. Then trust God for good things in the future.

4. Be thankful.
And finally, when all our happiness has leaked away it is often because we have made our happiness rely on only one situation –

the one that is a major downer right now. Tunnel vision makes us overlook many good things that we are taking for granted. Take your mind off what you are lacking for a moment. Be thankful for everything you already have, and it will refill your happiness tank.

TODAY'S CHALLENGE

1. **Eliminate Stinkin' Thinkin'**
   Are you wondering why joy is missing from your life, even though you are a Christian? Have you ever looked heavenward with a skeptical eye wondering why God isn't keeping His end of the bargain and making you happy? Well, me too sometimes. When we are waiting for God to inject some joy into our lives, we are forgetting that happiness is a fruit of the spirit that grows in us when our spiritual walk with God is healthy. Instead of looking for a double shot of happiness from God, look at your spiritual walk and see where happiness could be leaking.

2. **Initiate Awesome Actions**
   Write out the four action steps from Philippians 4 listed above on a card or on your phone or computer, where you can access it easily. When happiness starts leaking, take hold of the list and let the truths take hold of you by putting them into action.

Clark Gerhart

"Spiritual depth is not about what you know. It's about what you do with what you know."

With the help of a smart phone you can now create an entire fake life on social media. You can take a picture by a tree in your back yard and tell people you are hiking the Appalachian Trail. Take a selfie at just the right angle … or even photoshop a picture … to add some curves here … or take some away over there. You can post a picture from the gym and look like a fitness junkie, even if you never actually get on the treadmill. We all know people who *say* they do a whole lot more than they *actually* do. If you have a Facebook, I imagine that two or three names immediately came to mind. There's someone in every group. So, if nobody comes to mind, then I hate to be the one to break the news ... it might just be you.

With religion it's the same … maybe more so. I think we all know people who are far more concerned with talking about Christian principles than they are actually living them out. Now, I know learning theology is exciting and certain religious issues stir up passion in us. That's a good thing! It's rather easy to hear things, talk about them, and post about them. But what's *hard* is letting God highlight an issue in your life, working your butt off to *apply it,* and letting it genuinely change who you are.

Patience is one of those Christian traits that is easy to talk about but hard to do. On multiple occasions I observed Scott exercise what I perceived as supernatural amounts of patience in challenging situations. I was baffled as he'd stand by quietly while somebody ranted on with attacking religious nonsense. I remember asking him, "Why don't you just put an end to that crap and make them look silly? You're about a thousand times smarter than them!" He simply reminded me, "It's not about knowing more or winning an argument ... it's about using what you know to impact others. They're clearly not looking to grow right now and it's not my responsibility to force them. Don't waste your energy on that stuff … focus on your mission." He had a whole lot of spiritual info he could have dumped on them, but that wouldn't have helped them. So, he exercised patience.

That interaction shifted something in my heart. It was so freeing, yet so freaking challenging. Mostly because I personally struggle with something very similar: Pride. Knowing things (or communicating well enough to trick people into thinking I do) gives me pride. Especially when it means disarming some arrogant Christian who's trying to attack other people ... now THAT gets me going! Justice! There's just nothing like force-feeding bite size doses of humility like it's candy on Halloween. When in actuality, it's not some noble fight for justice ... *stop lying to yourself, Brooke.* Subconsciously this "silencing the mockers" is just me trying to gain value from knowledge instead of staying focused on the mission. It just meant that I was ALSO being an arrogant Christian, perhaps with a *bit* more subtleness. Now that's gross. It's a whole lot of great talk that hides a lack of real spiritual depth.

Behind the fake spiritual selfie that I create, what I actually see is God looking down and shaking His head at all of our human "knowledge." As if little Brookie comes running with his new drawing of Christianity ... colors of crayon spread across a paper … and says, "Look what a great Christian I am, Dad! And it's better than the rest of my class!" He leans to His right, where Jesus is comfortably seated, "Hey, look how adorable. *facepalm* Brooke thinks he knows everything."

You see, spiritual depth is more about simply being obedient to the Father's voice. In 1 John, notice that he did not instruct us to merely "know" more. He said that if we claim to live in God, then we need to obey His commands and *live as Jesus did.* That's it. It all comes back to

Jesus. You starting to catch a theme here? Less talk. More patience, humility, and love for others … all things Jesus actually *did.*

You want to get deeper in your spiritual life? Remember, that spiritual depth is not about what you know, it's about what you do with what you know. We need to shut our mouths and go do some Jesus stuff. And the next time you get prideful about how you know something better than someone else, remember that compared to God, you're barely coloring inside the lines. It's cute when you run your picture up to your Father, yelling, "Daddy look, I did this for you!" He adores those moments with you. Those go on the refrigerator in heaven! But when you shake that picture in someone else's face and brag about how much better yours is ... well, it's like us posting a fake selfie on Instagram to make people think we're wonderful.

> And we can be sure that we know him if we obey his commandments. If someone claims, "I know God," but doesn't obey God's commandments, that person is a liar and is not living in the truth. But those who obey God's word truly show how completely they love him. That is how we know we are living in him. Those who say they live in God should live their lives as Jesus did.
>
> 1 John 2: 3-6 (NLT)

We have a mission: To get out into the world and love people like Jesus does.

Let's DO that.

TODAY'S CHALLENGE

1. **Eliminate Stinkin' Thinkin'**
   The next time you are involved in a religious discussion, in person or online … especially online … think about what triggers your responses. Do you pursue spiritual knowledge with the intent of looking like a better Christian, maybe even showing that your spiritual selfie is better than other people's? Or, are you using what you know to better live like Jesus?

2. **Initiate Awesome Actions**
   If you ever get baited into a debate or feel "triggered" on Facebook because you know more than that troll, close the freaking app. Instead of sharing how much you know, DO something to impact them the way Jesus would. Show some patience, humility and love. Reply with something encouraging. You can also get off social media and out into the real world! Go serve at your local church or in your community. You'll be amazed at how much spiritual depth you *develop* when you're actually on the frontlines, being the hands and feet of Jesus.

Brooke Gerhart

"I'm not sure what direction God wants me to go next. And, I have a sense it doesn't really matter."

We were back at Jackie's. I was shoveling *Sh*t on a Shingle* (diner talk for creamed chipped beef on toast) into my mouth while Scott worked on some eggs. Scott had twenty-five years of experience as an operational leader and I had fifteen years of higher education. We were using that incredible combined decision-making power (wink) to evaluate Scott's next career move. Looking back, I imagine it must have resembled Winston Churchill and Franklin Roosevelt planning the invasion of Normandy. (Some would say more like Bill and Ted planning their next excellent adventure.) We examined the choices from every possible angle, identifying personal goals for the future and working toward a clear plan for success.

Finally, I wiped a bit of cream sauce from my chin and said, "So, which way do you think you'll go? Job A or job B?" Scott set down his fork, paused for a moment, then answered, "I'm not sure what direction God wants me to go next. And, I have a sense it doesn't really matter."

Just a few weeks later Scott was in heaven, and he was right. It didn't really matter.

Thinking back, I've wondered if Scott had some premonition of his death. It wouldn't be unheard of to walk closely with God and have His Spirit speak to you in quiet whispers about the path ahead. Yet, I know he didn't need a prophetic foretelling to recognize that his next step was ultimately nothing to worry about. Scott lived with an understanding that this life was not about him. Whether he succeeded or failed, lived or died, was immaterial. Accomplishing God's will was all that mattered.

While Scott and I were sitting there at Jackie's making decisions, God must have been in heaven chuckling and saying, "Why, you do not even know what will happen tomorrow. What is your life? You are a mist that appears for a little while and then vanishes. Instead, you ought to say, "If it is the Lord's will, we will live and do this or that.'" (James 4:13-15 NIV) Actually, I'm sure that's what Scott meant. He didn't know what life would hold tomorrow, but he did know that he would be pursuing what God really wanted, either way.

So, what does God want?

My brother Kent figured that out. At age fifty he found out he had stage four colon cancer which spread to his liver. That's bad news. With treatment, his chance of living more than 5 years was only about 25%. That's a 75% chance of dying! Pretty grim news for this husband and father of 3 young women. Kent was not worried, however. He was a Christian and knew where he was going. He even considered refusing treatment to help arrive at his eternal reward a little faster. He talked this over with his wife and … no need to wonder how that conversation went … he went through big surgery and grueling chemotherapy.

After two years the cancer in his liver was back, which meant back to the operating room. If the odds were grim before, they were dire now.

During all of that arduous treatment, Kent said there were many nights he realized, "I could die from this tonight!" That stark realization impacted him. Eventually, the CT scans and the blood tests started improving. The shock of, "What if I don't wake up tomorrow?" changed to, "What if I do?"

The answer became clear to Kent: Less focus on me and more on helping others experience God's love. Ten years later and disease free, Kent says, "Now my day usually starts with 'Ok Jesus, I woke up today on earth and not in heaven. What's the plan for today? Who will you put in my path today? Does the cashier at WaWa convenience store need a kind word? Is the employee in the next cubicle going through a tough situation? Can I pray for someone at Biggies (a local bar/diner where he hung out to meet people and talk about their spiritual lives)?'" He continues, "It's a matter of focus. Nothing different than anything else a Christian should say or do. Now it is just more real for me. I have found that on those days where I make this my posture and focus, things happen. Holy coincidences occur, and I can see God moving in people's lives."

Paul, who knew a lot about the ups and downs of following Christ, had the same outlook. He was in prison when he wrote to the Christians in Philippi to let them know that his odds of surviving were … well, probably not much better than 25%. He wasn't entirely sure what direction God was going to take him next. He also had a sense that it didn't really matter. He concluded that to live would be about sharing Christ more but to go to heaven would be good, too. Either way I'm cool with it, he says.

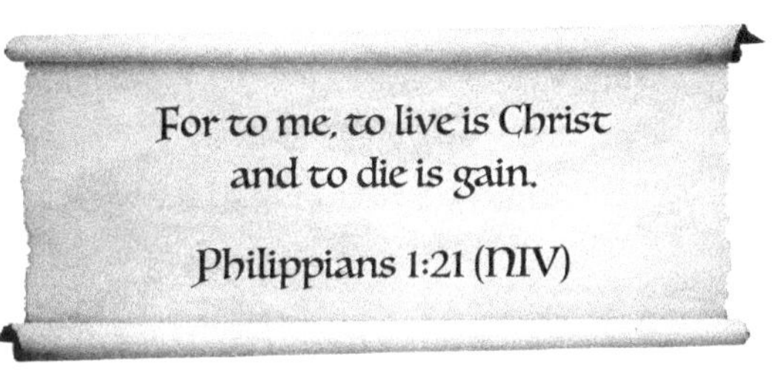

Since you're alive and reading this, God has determined that you don't get the "to die is gain" part. So, I guess you get the "to live is Christ" option. What does that mean for you?

I don't think you can fully answer that question until you face the reality of your death. Maybe that happens when you're in prison on death row, like Paul, or maybe when you get advanced cancer, like Kent. Or maybe you experience it through someone else, like when your best friend, somebody just like you, suddenly dies. We all live planning for tomorrow as if tomorrow will always arrive. But what if tomorrow doesn't? What if it does?

TODAY'S CHALLENGE

So, here's your final challenge. If you die tonight where will you go? If you wake up tomorrow, what will you do? Even now, I can hear Scott inviting … challenging! ... each of us to live a life committed to sharing the outrageous love of another kind wherever God's will takes us. Because then, when we face difficult choices, we will have peace in knowing it doesn't really matter.

Clark Gerhart

God loves you like crazy. Life is too short to worry about anything else.

Based on the quotes of
Scott Fetterolf

Proceeds from the sale of Outrageous Love will go to the Scott J. Fetterolf Memorial Scholarship Endowment at Lancaster Bible College

For more information or to donate visit:

https://lcbcchurch.com/scott-j-fetterolf-memorial-scholarship-endowment-page

Made in USA - North Chelmsford, MA
1033355_9780578585703
12.09.2019 1300